Land of Nakoda

THE STORY OF THE ASSINIBOINE INDIANS

From the tales of the Old Ones told to
First Boy (James L. Long)

With drawings by
Fire Bear (William Standing)

FEDERAL WRITERS' PROJECT

From the tales of the *Old Ones* told to First Boy (James L. Long),
with drawings by Fire Bear (William Standing),
under direction of the Writers' Program of the
Work Projects Administration in the State of Montana.

1942 State Publishing Company
Helena, Montana

Original elements of this edition copyright © 2004 by Riverbend Publishing.

Published by Riverbend Publishing, Helena, Montana.

Printed in the United States of America.

4 5 6 7 8 9 0 MG 20 19 18 17 16 15

Cover and text design by DD Dowden

ISBN 1-931832-35-8

Cataloging-in-Publication data is on file at the Library of Congress.

Riverbend Publishing
P.O. Box 5833
Helena, MT 59604
Toll-free 1-866-787-2363
www.riverbendpublishing.com

*Dedicated to a deeper appreciation of a
misunderstood and mistreated people:*

*The First Americans,
the North American Indians.*

Foreword

The *Land of Nakoda* is an important book—a book that presents memories of a way of life that will not be experienced again in the foreseeable future. The reprinting of this book is particularly important to the living Nakoda people, whose relatives survived generation after generation, with harmony and respect in a wonderful, but often harsh environment. The book has special meaning because it was written and illustrated by Nakoda men whose own lives extended into the nineteenth century and who had considerable knowledge of the land, language and culture of the people from whom the information was obtained.

The style of the book is simple and straightforward. It is a reflection of James L. Long and his empathy with those people who had lived the hard life on the plains. The descriptions of everyday life and the social structure that arises from that life are detailed and focused but at the same time hint at the subtlety of the spiritual essence and humbleness of man living in harmony with nature. The book reflects the respect shown by the interviewer for the truth and accuracy of the oral tradition, which provided these crucial details and stories for the book. It is the essence of Assiniboine culture that has been transmitted to modern times from the sons and daughters of the *Land of Nakoda*.

It is obvious that respect for oral tradition dominates the content of this book. Despite musing by anthropologists and historians about the origins, kinship and alliances of the Nakoda, that oral tradition has considered the Nakoda as a singular, unique people from long before contact with Europeans.

Fort Peck Community College is delighted and thankful that this essential book is being reprinted. It will enable students of the future to understand the lives and ways of their ancestors.

James Shanley
Stands in the Eagle Lodge
President, Fort Peck Community College

Contents

Foreword ... iv
Preface ... 1
From Earliest Times to the Present ... 3

PART I TRIBAL LEGENDS
How the Summer Season Came ... 10
Moon Calendar ... 13
Power of the Peace Pipe ... 17

PART II: TRIBAL LIFE
The Tribe ... 24
Camp Moving ... 29
Courtship and Marriage ... 37
Children ... 42
Crazy Dog Stories ... 51
War Parties ... 55
Dances and Social Gatherings ... 65

PART III: LODGES, FOOD AND GAMES
Buffalo—Staff of Life ... 74
Fire Making ... 86
Foods ... 88
The Old Woman Who Tricked Her Captors ... 94
Lodges, Clothing and Ornaments ... 96
Stone and Bone Articles ... 104
Games ... 107

PART IV: HUNTING
Bow and Arrows ... 112
The Tribal Hunt ... 116
Traps and Snares ... 123
The Chase ... 126
Story of Fast Runner ... 133
Hunting Deer ... 136

PART V: CEREMONIES AND SOCIETIES
Social and Secret Organizations … 140
Women's Dances … 143
The Grass Dance … 147
Medicine Lodge Dance … 169

PART VI: MEDICINE MEN AND SPIRITS
Men With Magic … 176
Death and the Spirit Bundle … 183
The Spirit World … 187
Journey of the Spirit … 190

PART VII: COMING OF THE WHITE MEN
The Ones Who Paddle a Canoe … 194
Lone White Man … 198
Meeting With the Sioux … 201
Treaties and Reservation Life … 204

PART VIII: APPENDICES
The Author … 213
The Illustrator … 217
The Old Ones Who Told the Stories … 221
Assiniboine Bands … 225
Pronunciation Key … 226
Pronunciation Guide for Months and Seasons … 227
Reading List … 228

Illustrations

Medicine Shield ... iii
Old time camp crier ... vi
Man with the whip ... ix
Ceremonial dancer ... x
A medicine lodge ... 2
Recounting big medicine... 3
Inside a warrior's lodge ... 5
Civilization comes to the Assiniboine ... 7
Cranes carry the Summer ... 8
Old men who guarded the Summer ... 10
Family groups argued the moon count ...13
Sign of bad weather ... 15
The moon "sits straight;" fair weather ... 16
People of the North see the spirit light ... 18
A decorated back rest ... 21
Camp life ... 24
Speech between Son-in-law and Mother-in-law was prohibited ... 26
Selection of a chieftain ... 28
Camp moving ... 30
Big Dog, the first horse ... 31
Dog travois ... 32
Horse travois ... 33
A bull boat ... 34
Tribulations of the dog travois era ... 35
Courtship—in reverse ... 37
Boys' sport: shooting mice ... 42
Navel bag ... 43
Baby's sleeping bag ... 44
A crazy dog ... 51
Treating a crazy dog victim ... 53
Return of the horse raiders ... 55
Making medicine for a war party ... 57
Counting coup on the enemy ... 60
On the warpath ... 62
The Grass Dance ... 65
A Grass Dancer ... 71
Buffalo herd ... 74

The chase ... 77

Sacred buffalo rock ... 82

Buffalo hide scraper ... 85

War party making fire ... 87

Preparing dried buffalo meat ... 88

War party cooking meat ... 90

The maiden who lied ... 91

Digging wild turnips ... 92

Picking juneberries ... 93

Pounding chokecherries ... 93

Old woman who tricked her captors ... 94

Buffalo hide lodge ... 96

Lodge construction details ... 99

Summer moccasins ... 101

Women's hair dress ... 102

Men's hair style ... 102

Making stone pipes ... 104

Stone war hammer ... 105

Types of stone pipes ... 106

Spinning buffalo horn tops ... 107

Positions of the slide stick game ... 109

Boy's mud stick game ... 110

Making bows and arrows ... 112

Bow, arrows and point types ... 114

The boy who saved his mother ... 115

Buffalo trap 116

Ceremony for successful buffalo hunt ... 118

Buffalo trap diagram... 120

Wolf skin disguise for wintertime hunting ... 122

Building a small game trap ... 123

Rabbit snare ... 124

Catching young ducks ... 125

Buffalo chase ... 126

The hunter's escape ... 128

Buffalo horse saves his rider ... 129

Where Slanting ran a buffalo herd over the cutbank ... 130, 131

Successful hunter's return ... 131

Deer Society wrist charm ... 132

Warrior wearing Deer Society costume ... 132

Cloud outruns an antelope ... 133

Deer hunting by moonlight ... 136
Deer hunting in winter ... 137
Boys Act Like Dogs Society ... 140
Kit Fox Society headpiece ... 141
Female Elk Dance ... 143
Ceremonial drum ... 144
Ceremony for a successful hunt ... 146
The Grass Dance ... 148
Grass Dancer in full costume ... 149
Headdress of a grass dancer ... 150
Young dancer with a forked spit ... 155
Grass Dance Belt Ceremony ... 162
Medicine Lodge Dance ... 169
Lovers brought the Medicine Pole ... 171
Medicine Pole and dancer ... 174
Men with magic ... 176
Medicine man ... 177
Medicine charm ... 178
Medicine symbol ... 179
Bear claw charm ... 180
Medicine man performing ... 182
Tree burial ... 183
The death watch ... 186
Making medicine over the dying ... 187
Visit to the spirit world ... 188
Outside the death lodge ... 189
Battle with a Piegan ... 190
The ones who paddle a canoe ... 194
First meeting with the white men ... 197
Lone white man ... 198
Feeding the refugee Sioux ... 201
Sioux from the Minnesota massacre ... 203
Assiniboine become farmers ... 204
Bear's 40-acre allotment ... 206
Blue Cloud's land ... 207
Indian policemen ... 208
Picture writing (the Author) ... 212
Painting lodge designs (The Illustrator) ... 217
Recounting big medicine ... 221

PREFACE

THIS BOOK ATTEMPTS TO RECORD AND SAVE—before the passing of the last of the Old Ones capable of providing it—the Assiniboine's own story of their life in the few centuries preceding the encroachment of the white man's "civilization."

The story is told in the Indian's straight-forward way, without flourish or embellishment, by James L. Long (First Boy) and illustrated with original drawings by William Standing (Fire Bear).

In compiling the notes and conducting the field research Mr. Long used original sources, chiefly interviews with the oldest members of the tribe. Only when a controversial matter could not be authenticated or clarified by the old Indians—most of whom have since died—were published books, papers and reports on the Assiniboine referred to by Mr. Long or the editors.

The pen and ink illustrations of William Standing, supplementing the word-of-mouth versions told almost entirely in the Assiniboine tongue by the Old Ones and recorded by Mr. Long, constitute a sympathetic, accurate and graphic record of the Assiniboine which should increase in value with every passing year.

Special acknowledgment therefore is made to Mr. Long and Mr. Standing as members of the staff of the WPA Writers' and Art Projects, respectively. These two projects have served, as we hope they may continue to serve, in directing the recording of such priceless word-of-mouth stones as these before they completely perish with the passing of our oldest Indians.

Special thanks for assistance are also due Mr. L. E. Larson, Ralph Henry, Alvin Warrior, Mrs. Margaret Whitaker, Frank L. Stevens, State Supervisor of the Montana WPA Art Project, and many others who assisted in this work.

This is the first of a series of books about the Indians planned by the Montana Writers' Project. Others are to be prepared dealing with the Blackfoot, Flathead, Crow, Gros Ventre, Northern Cheyenne, Cree, Fort Belknap Assiniboine and the Rocky Boy Chippewa. They will be compiled in what seems to be the only logical method for such work—allowing the Indian to write and illustrate his own story. This book seeks to preserve for our own and future generations, both Indian and white, an authentic picture of Indian life. These stories, almost without exception, would have been irrevocably lost if they had not been gathered and written down. Many of the Assiniboine already no longer talk the language of their people and their children will know less of their ancestors. It is hoped that the stories and legends the old men and women so gladly and freely told will interest both Assiniboine and white readers, and that because of this book the Assiniboine may be known, respected, and better understood.

MICHAEL KENNEDY, Supervisor, Montana Writers' Project

From Earliest Times to the Present

IN THE MEMORY OF THE OLDEST LIVING ASSINIBOINE, based on what he remembers from his oldest ancestor, who in turn was told the story by those "old ones far back," the tribe of Nakoda lived "in a land always covered with snow."

The ethnologists go beyond that. It is conjectured that before the coming of the white man to this continent, the Assiniboine lived quite a different life far to the southeast as the Nakton branch of the vast Siouan Nation. Before the seventeenth century they may have been the northernmost vanguard of a migration which, over a period of centuries, moved from the warmer climate up into what is now the area between Illinois and eastern North Dakota.

In recorded history, the Assiniboine, who call themselves Nakoda's People, meaning people not at war, are mentioned by the early Jesuits as a distinct and robust tribe living in the forest and lake region around Lake Winnipeg in 1610. Father Claude Jean Allouez sixteen years later wrote that they had long been known to the French. When a permanent trading post on Hudson's Bay was founded in 1670,

some adventurous Assiniboine, along with the Cree, were there to trade. From this date barter with the whites was carried on. Some guns, metal utensils and a few of the white man's trinkets then came into use for the first time.

The doughty French adventurer, Sieur de la Verendrye, who visited the Assiniboine in 1737 thought that they were divided into two groups. The woodland tribes to the north hunted fur-bearing animals for trade with the French. The plains tribes farther south were less affected by contact with the whites until some years later. The woodland Assiniboine, it seems, were the middlemen. They bought corn, squash, colored buffalo robes, furs, feathers and similar items from the Mandan village tribes on the Missouri River; in turn trading them for axes, knives, powder, bullets and guns from the French and the English.

By the middle of the eighteenth century the horse had been brought to the plains Assiniboine. But they were one of the last plains tribe to have the animal and it was not until the white man had quite thoroughly occupied the country that the horse replaced the dog as a beast of burden.

The thriving fur trade drew the woodland and plains groups more closely together until by the nineteenth century there were few major differences. Some woolen goods had already appeared in their articles of dress. The white man's whiskey—a scourge worse than smallpox the Redman—was being introduced and accepted.

By 1839 (which was within the living memory of at least two tribe members at the time this book was begun) the Assiniboine were firmly established as an American tribe, living throughout northeastern Montana and northwestern North Dakota.

In that year sixty lodges came over from Canada to join their datives around Fort Union. Hunters moved south of the Missouri River to the hostile Crow country along the Yellowstone and west to the country of the fierce Blackfoot beyond the Sweet Grass Hills.

For the most part, the mode of life of the people, as recorded here the stories told by the old members of the tribe, undoubtedly represents the period from residence around Lake Winnipeg to 1839.

By the end of the Civil War, guns and metal knives had become almost indispensable. The white man's kettles, awls, tools for hide dressing and even firesteels were being used. Luxury items included scarlet blankets, gaudy calico and woolen shirts, white Hudson's Bay blankets, neckerchiefs, black silk handkerchiefs, cotton trousers, black fur hats, scarlet laced chief's coats and silver hat and arm bands. The traders were then living with the Indians, marrying their women, learning their ways and teaching them the white man's. River boats plied the Missouri to further confuse a way of life that was centuries old.

First Fly and Crazy Bear, representing all of the Assiniboine, signed the far-teaching Treaty of Fort Laramie on September 17, 18:51, between the United States Government and the chiefs and headmen of the Sioux, Cheyenne, Arapahoe, Crow, Gros Ventre, Mandan, Arikara and the Assiniboine Nations. This treaty marked the first cession of lands by the Assiniboine as well as the creation of the original reservation and the first chieftain with authority over the entire tribe. In order to facilitate negotiation, Crazy Bear, who participated with First Fly in negotiating the treaty, was elevated by the Treaty Commissioners to the post of Tribal Chief.

The first reservation area, described in detail elsewhere in this book, roughly covered all of northern Montana east of the Sweet Grass Hills and north of a line from the mouth of the Musselshell to the mouth of the Powder River, then up and across the northwest corner of North Dakota.

Four years later, under a treaty with the Blackfoot, the land ranging west from the mouth of Milk River to a point near present-day Havre was made common hunting grounds. In the decade following, the Blackfoot used this territory less and less and finally abandoned it to the Gros Ventre, Assiniboine, and the River Crow. In 1868 the latter

left to join the Mountain Crow south of the Yellowstone River, leaving the territory to the Gros Ventre and Assiniboine.

It was within the boundaries of this territory in 1873 that the Fort Belknap Reservation was set up following subdivision of the Milk River Reservation. The eastern part became the Fort Peck reserve, with Lower Assiniboine and Yanktonai Sioux as residents. The western part, or old Fort Belknap Reservation, with an agency then at a site below the present town of Chinook, was occupied by Gros Ventre and Northern Cheyenne.

Ten years later the buffalo was virtually extinct. With the passing of this major source of livelihood came the beginning of a new, strange and for the most part an unhappy way of life for all the Assiniboine.

At Fort Belknap they were compelled to settle down in 1884-85 just as they already had at Fort Peck. In that year the remainder of the northern band came down from Canada to settle permanently and over a hundred and fifty log cabins were built at Fort Belknap.

Farming was still in its initial stage, with most of the work performed by the women. But, nevertheless, it was beginning. Pressure was now being brought to bear by government officials against the performance of such time-honored rituals as the Sun-Dance and other ceremonials. Agency day schools and church missions were established. Cattle—the white man's buffalo—had been introduced, to replace the shaggy ruminants.

By 1880 the old way of life of the Assiniboine was drastically changed. Farming and stock raising were occupations for which they were totally unprepared. Cabin homes and the Government's food money allotments were strange innovations. Schools and missions made deeper inroads into the framework of the old culture. Whites were arriving in ever-increasing numbers to do business and to further intermarry. In 1908 the total Assiniboine population was placed at 2,090, almost a seventy-five per cent decrease since 1832.

Contact with whites and the schools brought the inevitable reaction among the younger generation—a feeling that the "old way" of life was outmoded, primitive or inferior. Those who attempted to live in the traditional way were put on the defensive. Frequently they were compelled to reinterpret the symbolism of their old religions ceremonies into terms that were at least part of the white man's culture.

"Civilization" had come to the Assiniboine.

"Cranes carry the Summer"

PART I

TRIBAL LEGENDS

How the Summer Season Came

Moon Calendar

Power of the Peace Pipe

How the Summer Season Came

A LONG TIME AGO, the Assiniboine people were in country almost always covered with snow. There were no horses and only dogs were used to carry things.

A small war party, that had been gone a long time, returned and went at once to the chief's lodge. They told him to call his counsellors together for they had an important message. The chief set food before them and sent his camp crier to call the council members to his lodge.

The spokesman said, "We have been away from our people for many moons. We have set foot on land that belongs to others; we have set foot on land without snow. It is in the direction of where the sun rests at midday.

"In the middle of a large encampment there is a lodge painted yellow. In this the summer is kept in a bag hung on a tripod. Four old men guard it day and night. One sits in the back, directly under the tripod; another lies across the entrance and two others sit on each side of the fireplace."

The chief and his headmen sat in council until one of them said, "Let us call in a representative of each kind of the fast running animals and ask them to help us bring this wonderful thing to our country." So the camp

"SUMMER IS IN A BAG ... FOUR OLD MEN GUARD IT NIGHT AND DAY ..."

crier went forth and called to those medicine men, who had fast running animals for their helpers, to invite them to the lodge.

When all were in council the chief said, "My people and my brothers (the animals), far in the direction of midday there is the summer and I call you here to make plans to bring it to our people. The ones who go will never come back alive but they will do a great good to our people and their kind; for their children will enjoy the breath of the summer forever."

It was decided to send the Lynx, the Red Fox, the Antelope, the Coyote and the Wolf. The young warriors, who knew the way, were to guide the runners to the encampment.

After many days' march they arrived near the camp and took council. The spokesman said, "The Lynx will go into the lodge and bring out the bag containing the summer, because nobody can hear him walk. He will give it to the Red Fox, who will be waiting for him along the way. From there, the Antelope will carry it to the Coyote, who will take it to the Wolf who is long-winded, and he will bring it to us by the big river, where we will be waiting on the opposite bank. From there we will take it to our people."

So, the Lynx was left there and the rest went back in the direction from which they had come.

The Red Fox first was told to take his position, and so on until all the animals were stationed a certain distance apart according to the ability of the runner. If an animal was short-winded, it was not required to make a long run, for the bag was to be carried at the fastest speed.

Towards morning, before the light showed and when slumber was in every lodge, the Lynx softly walked to the yellow lodge and looked in. The four old men were all asleep. The bag, containing the summer, was hanging on the tripod in the back part of the lodge.

The summer was in the form of spring water. It moved about in a bag made from the stomach of a buffalo. Now and then it overflowed and trick-led along the ground, under the tripod, and in its wake green grass and many different kinds of plants and flowers grew luxuriantly. Cautiously, on stealthy feet, the Lynx entered, stepping over the entrance and, with a quick jerk, snapped the cord that held the bag. Seizing it tightly in his teeth, he plunged through the door and sped away.

Almost the same instant the old men awakened and gave the alarm: "The summer has been stolen!" The cry went from lodge to lodge and in a short time a group on fast horses were after the Lynx.

They were fast gaining on the Lynx when he gave the bag to the Red Fox who was waiting. The horsemen then killed the Lynx and started after the Fox who, after a time, gave the bag to the Antelope. The Antelope took it to the Coyote, who brought it to the Wolf, the long-winded one, who was to deliver it to the waiting party. Each time the bag was passed to the next runner, the winded animal was killed by the pursuers.

The fast horses were tired but gained steadily on the Wolf. As he sped across the country, the snow melted away directly behind him; grass sprang up green; trees and bushes unfolded their leaves as summer passed by. Fowls seemed to join the pursuit, as flock after flock flew northward.

As the Wolf crossed the river the ice moved and broke up. By the time the horsemen reached it, the river was flowing bank-full of ice. This halted the Southern people. In sign language they said to the Assiniboine, "Let us bargain with each other for the possession of the summer." After a time it was decided that each would keep the summer for six moons. Then it was to be taken back to the river and delivered to the waiting party.

That agreement was kept, so there was summer half of the year in each country. In that way there were the two seasons, the winter and summer.

After many two-season years had passed, the headmen of the Assiniboines decided to have the cranes carry the summer back and forth. They were always the first of the migratory fowl to go south. They moved by easy stages, stopping for long periods at good feeding grounds. That method of carrying the summer, the winter gradually followed cranes, so that, instead of the sudden winter as when the summer was taken south by the men, the fall season, *Pdanyedu,* made its appearance. Long before the cranes returned, there were signs among the plants and animals that the summer was on its way north. That time was called the spring, *Wedu.*

A late fall or spring was a sign that the cranes had found good feeding grounds and tarried there too long. An early winter or summer was a sign that the carriers had winged their way south or north in haste.

As the cranes flew over an encampment they always circled several times and, with their loud calls, seemed to proclaim their arrival or departure.

So, finally, the Assiniboine had four seasons: the winter, *Waniyedu;* summer, *Mnogedu;* the fall, *Pdanyedu,* and the spring, *Wedu.*

Moon Calendar

The Assiniboine always had a twelve-moon calendar.

January was *Wicogandu*, Center Moon, because October to April was allotted to the winter season. Therefore. January was the halfway mark and considered the big moon. It was also called, *Witehi*. This meant, Hard Moon or Hard Time Moon, on account of the severe cold weather during that period.

Due to the sap freezing, cottonwood trees burst with loud reports in that moon, which was a sign the Center Moon was on duty.

There was always a question at that time of the year, has to the correct count of the moon. Groups were pitted against each other in argument; and even a man and wife would disagree and take sides.

Those that counted in error never admitted it, even after signs in that moon were brought to their attention.

That sort of gentle family argument continued through the winter moons until spring when it gradually died away only to come up again the next winter.

February was *Amhanska*, Long Day Moon. The days lengthened in that moon.

March was *Wicinstayazan*, Sore-eye Moon. Snow blindness was common during that period.

April, *Tabehatawi*, Frog's Moon. The croaking of the frogs was heard in that moon.

May, *Induwiga*, Idle Moon. The winter season was over and there was a pause before summer began.

June, *Waheqosmewi*, Full Leaf Moon. All leaves reached their full growth in that moon.

July, *Wasasa*, Red Berries Moon.

August, *Capasapsaba*, Black Cherries Moon. Chokecherries ripened in that moon.

September, *Wahpegiwi*, Yellow Leaf Moon.

October, *Tasnaheja-hagikta*, The Stripped Gopher Looks Back. There were summer-like days in that moon. The supposition was that the gopher, although in its hibernation, came out to have a last look at the fine weather. That animal was often seen out after the full moon. It was also called, *Anukope*, Joins both Sides, which meant part summer and part winter, because there was warm and cold weather in that moon. So the moon was a dividing line between summer and winter.

November, *Cuhotgawi*, Frost Moon. In that moon the heavy frost covered the leafless trees, bushes and the landscape; the early morning air glistened as the sun rose. November was rightly named.

December was *Wicogandu-sungagu*, Center Moon's Young Brother.

Because January was considered the big moon, December was a young brother who clung to his older brother.

Old men kept account of the days in a moon by notching on their pipe cleaners, one notch for one day. These pipe cleaners were made from a small willow the size of a pencil and about a foot long.

A row of notches the length of a pipe cleaner would constitute a moon period, or a month. One of those sticks notched down four sides counted four months and three fully notched sticks made a full year.

The days in a moon were counted by watching the moon in its various positions and adding two more days, which were the days that the moon was not visible.

The last two days of an old moon, when not visible were referred to as, "The moon hides, because it is going to die."

The first two days of a new moon were called, "The moon does not come," meaning, the new moon was now on duty and was making preparations for its appearance.

If the weather was fair or unsettled during the two days that the old moon was "dying", and continued in that state through the first two days of the new moon, then fair or unsettled weather would prevail until the new moon's first quarter.

On the third evening of the new moon period, if the sky was clear, the moon "Sits in" and was visible in a faint outline. Its position would precast the weather for that moon's rule.

If it "Sits straight," that is, if the tips were in a perpendicular position, then the moon brought forth chiefly fair days and if it "Lays on its back," it was a sign of bad weather.

When the new moon was "Leaning back," there was an equal amount of fair and unsettled weather.

There were, as said before, four seasons: *Waniyedu,* winter; *Wedu,* spring; *Mnogedu,* summer; *Pdanyeda,* fall.

The principle seasons were the winter and the summer. The Winter was used for determining the ages of people like, "He is thirty winters," meaning, thirty years old. "Ten winters ago," for ten years ago. If the birth was in summer, then they said, "He will be thirty winters this summer."

The moons that belong to the winter season were, October, November, December, January, February, March and April. These were moons in which there was no growth, no berries or fruit and the tops of root plants like the turnip, a food plant, and different plants used for medicine were dead and blown away.

Therefore, as the winter has two more moons, it was always considered the principal reckoning season.

Power of the Peace Pipe

LONG AGO THE *WAZIYAMWINCASTA*, PEOPLE OF THE NORTH, one of the many bands that formed the great Assiniboine tribe, were camped in the northern part of their territory, in the land claimed by the Red Coats (British).

It was in the Joins both Sides moon and the weather during that moon was always much loved by the people, because the days were still summer but the nights whispered the coming of winter.

The buffaloes were moving in the direction where the sun reaches halfway on its daily journey. The people had already put much cured meat away for the cold season and soon they would leisurely follow the buffaloes as far as the Cypress Hills, their winter camp grounds.

The people were all in camp, as the big hunting season was about over; no war parties were out so there was rest and peace. Only the laughter of children was heard while at play. It was the time when women were in their lodges making clothing for the cold that was sure to come. The men, too, were busy on new bows, arrows and other things to be made from different kinds of wood now matured. Those men sat outside their lodges or took their work to another's place to work and visit as well. Some old men and women made extra travois to pack the cured meats and berries when moving time came.

There was no need for hurried tasks as the stripped-back gopher still frolicked about, a sign that summer would linger yet awhile.

Since this long ago time the snow has fallen many, many winters, so many that only the very old remembered the story as it was told to them by the ones who were there. They say:

It seemed like a skilled hunter was ready to make the kill, so quietly did it happen and so unsuspecting was the victim.

A man, who sat near his lodge, busy at a task, spoke to his wife, who was within. "There is a medicine man going into the lodge of the chief. Have you heard if anyone there is ill?" "I am sure no one is ill. It may be that he is asked to eat with the chief," was the answer. But soon camp talk reached around that Comes Out Chief, only child of the chief, was taken suddenly ill. "He was just playing with the other children this morning," the old grandfather had said of the six-year old boy.

Soon noted medicine men gathered in the lodge of the chief; not of their own accord, but each one was given gifts and entreated to come. Before the next morning the spirit of little Comes Out Chief had departed to join his only and older sister, who died some years before. There was much sorrow in the camp and the heart of Takes The Weapon, the chief, was heavy. He cut deep gashes on his arms, legs and body as an act of mourning. He refused to be taken to the guest lodge; he wanted to be near the body of the boy, which reposed in the arms of the mother in their own lodge. He cried, "No, my son is still here, for the spirits do not leave the encampment until four days have passed. They always wait for the feast that is prepared for them and then take their departure. It is well that I remain here."

The headmen went in a body to the chief's lodge and sat with him. One of the servers first told of a war deed, then he took the chief's sacred bundle from its place on a tripod. On live embers from the fire he placed pieces of dried sweet grass which he broke off from a long braided coil. He took the

THE SPIRIT OF COMES OUT CHEIF …
"A WHITE LIGHT, WAS NOTICED BY THE PEOPLE …"

bundle and passed it back and forth, four times, over the smoke offering. He filled it with tobacco and lit it with a piece of live ember. After a few puffs he extended the mouthpiece toward the chief and bade him smoke.

"Once," he said, "this pipe has made you happy. That was when you became chief. It now can soothe you and bring your mind back to your people. Talk to us that we may know your wishes."

The chief took the pipe and with his right hand felt of the bowl and other parts in a caressing manner. He closed his eyes and drew deeply on the pipe. Many thoughts passed through his mind, thoughts that brought memories of when he was presented with that very pipe to hold sacred. He had been a good servant of the pipe; he was always kind and generous to his people. Yes, that was what the server had said, "it will bring your mind back to your people." It was one of the times when the power of the pipe became the leader. It was well that its leadership be followed by its keeper.

After a time the silence was broken by the chief, who said, "Everyone knows that not all can reach gray hairs. But being that the pipe has come to me from my father and through three generations before him, it has always been my wish that when my son reached the age of deep thinking then my people might look toward him and honor him with the pipe. His grandfather on his mother's side has always told him many things and much of that remains with him, as you all know. Everyday I have offered food and the pipe to the spirits of his grandfathers that they may see and watch over him. You, my people and my relations, as you see me now I am alone with my wife; our family has come to an end; the pipe can no longer go to a keeper in our family: allow that it be presented to my boy as if he had reached the age of leadership. Leave me now and talk it over among yourselves while I mourn." The group voiced approval and went back to the guest lodge.

They talked and planned the best way to console their chief. Their minds were as one. "Send for Wounded Arm," they said, "the pipeman, the giver of pipes to headmen. He is the man who makes chiefs. He has been given that power on account of his many brave deeds in battles. His sacrifices to the Beings are many and his gifts to the poor are known even to other bands."

So a messenger was sent and the pipe-man accompanied him back to the guest lodge. He was a noble man, this giver of pipes, tall and kindly, who always wore a smile. Wounded Arm was an example to prospective chiefs and headmen that kindness made leaders.

A lodge was pitched near the guest lodge. Then the group went for the body of little Comes Out Chief. They brought it back and laid it in the honored place. A ceremony was performed the same as if the prospective one was living, only not a new pipe but the one handed down through the boy's family was used. At the end of the ceremony the pipe was laid on the body, with the bowl toward the foot. Then the body and the pipe were wrapped together to make the sacred bundle.

Never before had a bundle been made like that one, but the pipeman gave the instructions so the people were not afraid.

The headman took charge of the burial, which was high up in a tall tree. An untanned hide was wrapped over the body and made secure to the limbs. Then the people moved a short distance away in the direction of Cypress Hills, their winter home.

When darkness spread over the encampment, a white light, which extended upward over the burial tree, was noticed by the people. They gathered in groups and were amazed at the strange sign; they wondered at its meaning. Not knowing what else to do, they burned sweet grass on live embers as an offering and many medicine pipes were raised towards it.

The pipeman with several from the guest lodge went toward it and found the light remained over the burial. To be sure, they circled around to the north of it and back to camp. They told the people that the light came from the sacred bundle.

The people continued to move slowly away from the burial place. At night the strange light appeared and each time it extended a little higher. The feast for the dead was held and that night the light rose higher than ever before until its tip remained directly over the camp. After that no more was seen of it for many moons and, then, only at times.

"The ways of the Beings are wise," the people said, "they have placed little Comes Out Chief in the far north where he can look after us and be chief forever. With the peace pipe, he makes signs to us and we must offer many sacrifices; also erect sweat lodges so our medicine men can fast and purify themselves that they may be shown the meaning of the signs."

When the headmen were in council, the old chief, the father, never sat in the honored place. The decorated backrest was placed there and the spirit bundle, containing the lock of hair of the boy, was hung on it. The council relied a great deal on the spirit bundle, because it spoke to them by signs in the north that always were good for them. The people never failed to look northward at night because without warning the light might appear. Sometimes there were many lights on each side and when that happened Comes Out Chief had much to tell his people. Once he warned them to flee far northward toward him, away from the smallpox that came up the Missouri River. In its wake, many other bands perished, but not this one.

The People of the North invented the buffalo trap. They prospered. Their traps were always successful and the herds were large and came in quietly, because the spirit of Comes Out Chief joined them in the buffalo lodge from where the buffaloes were called. They became a large band and many more headmen were added to the council, but the back rest in the guest lodge was always reserved for the little spirit chief, who guided his people with the light that shone from the peace pipe.

"Comes Out Chief's place in the council of headmen was vacant ... but his spirit governed the tribe ..."

PART II
TRIBAL LIFE

The Tribe

Camp Moving

Courtship and Marriage

Children

Crazy Dog Stories

War Parties

Dances and Social Gatherings

The Tribe

IN THE VERY EARLY DAYS THE WHOLE ASSINIBOINE TRIBE of Indians was in one band. As the population increased the distribution of game, killed for meat, became a problem. There were complaints from families who did not get their share and often there was not enough to reach every lodge.

It was for that reason that families, with their near relatives, gradually moved away from the main band. They roamed and hunted as they chose, even though there was the danger of an attack from the enemy. As these small groups increased in size they naturally formed separate bands.

In time there were enough people in each band to set up the different societies and have their own dances and other amusements. A chief and headman finally made a band complete.

The separate groups lived alone and each occupied a district. The different locations of the bands brought about many new habits; and costumes were adopted which were most suitable to the country occupied. In that way the habits and costumes differed among the bands. While those who moved away were looked upon by the original band as deserters, there was still a friendly feeling between them.

As it formed into a regular band, each group was given a name by the people who did not move away. Some of the names suggested the kind of country the people lived in, such as *Ptegambina*, Swamp People; *Osnibi*, People of the Cold; and *Hebina*, Rock Mountain People. Other bands were given names to ridicule or reprimand them for their dress or habits of living such as *Cantidada,* Moldy People; or *Wazinazinyibi,* Fat Smokers.

The only way an estimate of the population of the tribe was made, before the white man came, was to count the bands and the number of people in each band. At the peak of their population the Assiniboine tribe consisted of thirty-three bands which had from 700 to 1,000 persons in each band.

In 1823 Renville estimated the number at 28,000 (7,000 warriors and 3,000 lodges). By 1908 Curtis placed the Assiniboine population at 1,217 in the U. S. and 873 in Canada.

When the bands were settled in their respective districts, the whole country was occupied. By this time the territory claimed by the Assiniboine was described in a suit against the United States Government. Their land lay within a line beginning on the South slope of the west end of the Little Rocky Mountains and running down the Missouri to the Musselshell River, across to the mouth of the Powder River, east along the north bank of the Yellowstone River to its mouth on the Missouri River, down the Missouri to where the White Earth empties into the Missouri, up along the west bank of the White Earth River to where it begins, north to the 49th parallel, which is the northern boundary of the United States today, west to a place north of the end of the Sweet Grass Hills, south to the east end of the Sweet Grass Hills, then southeast to the Little Rocky Mountains. This area was reduced more than half in the treaty of 1851.

The Assiniboine language was spoken among all of the bands. But those that occupied the northern and northwestern parts of the country which extended into Canada spoke with an accent that distinguished them from the Missouri River bands.

The women's speech was distinctly feminine. The pronunciation of many words differed from that of the men. They also used words not used by men. Therefore, the men avoided that kind of speech, because they did not wish to be accused of "talking like a woman."

Speech between father-in-law and daughter-in-law and between mother-in-law and son-in-law was strictly prohibited. Conversation was allowed between the two men and between the two women, but only in the third person plural and in a soft tone of voice, to show respect. They never spoke directly to each other, but always in a roundabout fashion.

One chief did not rule over the whole tribe. Each band had its own chief.

If the band was large, there were as many as three chiefs and many headmen. The headmen with the chief or chiefs formed the council.

A chief's son was not always the next chief. A person who had made a name for himself in warfare, hunting and kindness to the poor, was often made next chief. Sometimes a person known throughout the band as a medicine man, skilled in herb and magic and feared by the ruling class as well as the people, was made a chief.

A chief of that kind was not always chosen by the headmen of their own will, but through fear of the man. He may have expressed his desire for that position to one or more members who were in his power and they, because of their rank, executed his wishes.

Oftentimes a medicine-man chief was a bad ruler. He obtained the position because of his reputation as a person who could charm and throw different objects, such as the claws of animals and birds, into a person's body to cause sickness and possible death; or because he was able to perform visible magic before the people. At his wish, it was believed, he could call back the objects with which he charmed or afflicted others.

"SPEECH BETWEEN MOTHER-IN-LAW AND SON-IN-LAW WAS STRICTLY PROHIBITED."

At a council of the chiefs and headmen the subject of selecting another chief was brought to the attention of the members by one who had observed some likely person for a long time. He pointed out to the group the war and hunting record, also the family life of the man.

The requirements were that a chief-to-be must have a good war record, be a successful hunter, possessor of many horses for domestic use, and fast horses for use as buffalo runners. He must also, at least on one occasion, have brought back an enemy's scalp and presented it to his mother-in-law. On his hunting trips he must kill more game than his household required, so that he might distribute the surplus to the poor.

When a new chief was suggested the council talked the matter over. If they arrived at a favorable decision, the group went in a body, singing, to the prospective chief's lodge and the spokesman delivered the message. Not all the ones chosen accepted the position offered them. Sometimes one, not willing to be chief, if aware of the plan beforehand, departed on a hunting trip or visited at another band until the matter was dropped because of his absence. But if the offer was accepted the man was called outside. The group spread a tanned robe on the ground and the man was asked to take a seat in the middle of it. He was carried in that fashion to a new lodge that was pitched beside the guest lodge.

When the party arrived, they seated their guest in the back part of the new lodge and the ceremony began. They dressed him in new buckskin clothing and placed the sacred headgear on his head. That was a wide band cut from the tanned hide of a rare white buffalo and trimmed with small white beads. Then his face was painted with a narrow red stripe, starting at the right temple and extending upward along the hairline and across the brow to the left temple similar to the shape of a horse shoe. A short bar was painted on each end of the stripe.

A man whose whole body was painted red and who wore only a clout and moccasins was seated at the front of the lodge near the doorway. Before him were laid two black stone pipes, one with a plain wooden stem painted red. The stem of the other pipe was wrapped with quills in decorative colors from the mouthpiece halfway to the bowl. The mouthpiece was also wrapped with green-feathered skin, taken from the neck of a mallard drake. A small cluster of horse mane, dyed red, was attached to the lower end of the stem. A string of eagle tailfeathers, spaced about two inches apart, was fastened halfway down under the stem and extended to the end, near the bowl.

The singers started a song to which the pipeman danced, with the feathered pipe in his right hand. He danced forward and when in front of the guest he waved the pipe gently back and forth four times over the head of the future chief. Then the song stopped suddenly and the dancer walked back to his place, where he stood until the song was started again. The same procedure was repeated four times.

After that the old chief took the headgear off the guest, and, with the two pipes, a bundle was made and presented to the new chief as his sacred bundle. He was also given the new lodge and many horses. He was expected to present gifts, in return, to each of the chiefs and headmen at some future time.

"... AT A COUNCIL OF THE CHIEFS AND HEADMEN THE SUBJECT OF SELECTING ANOTHER CHIEF WAS BROUGHT TO THE ATTENTION OF THE MEMBERS...."

Camp Moving

AS THE TRIBE LIVED BY THE HUNT, they moved from place to place within their territory.

When the Assiniboine were farther North and before they had horses, each family had from six to twelve dogs capable of carrying up to fifty pounds each. They were used to pull the travois. As the women did all the tasks about the lodges, they named all the dogs. They spoke to them like persons, either scolded them or praised them whenever the dogs deserved it. Oftentimes, on a move, the dogs took after game and sometimes the entire load was upset, and left out on the prairie. When the dogs finally came back they were scolded and sometimes whipped.

It is told that, on one of those occurrences, a woman got so angry she whipped her dog until the dog turned on her. Several men, who were traveling parallel with the party, saw what was happening and ran to aid the woman but before they got there the dog killed her and ran away. The men gave chase, and the dog climbed a big hill where it sat down on the very top. When the pursuers were near, the dog disappeared beyond the hill. Although the men hunted in all directions the dog was nowhere to be seen.

For many years after, whenever a party passed by that hill, the dog could be seen sitting on top and after a time rose and slowly went beyond out of sight. One time a war party planned to surround the hill and kill the dog but when they ran up the hill from all directions the dog vanished. When each told of seeing the dog disappear over the hill from where they ascended, they were amazed and said. "It is the spirit of the dog. Perhaps no one would own it in the spirit world because it killed a human being. It came back to live in the hill near where the body of its mistress lies. Let us not disturb the will of the Beings who have done this."

The hill was known as the home of the travois dog.

One northern band, named Camp Movers to the Kill, never owned many dogs and when the men killed game they butchered it and sent word back to camp for the whole band to move up to the kill.

All of the fuel was gotten by the women and brought to camp by dog travois. The old women, with their dogs, went into the timber and loaded the travois for the dogs and then carried a load on their backs as well.

The aged, who could not travel with the band on foot, and small children rode travois. Two dogs hitched to their travois were placed side by side and the two centerpieces of the travois were fastened together with poles tied across both of them. A short stick was also tied between the necks of the travois to keep the dogs at a certain distance from each other. An old man or woman sat or laid on the cross pieces which held the two travois together. In that way, the load was drawn as one by both dogs.

Another way is told by Bad Hawk:

"One winter our band moved to another camping place and, as my old grandfather was unable to walk, three grown boys and myself pulled on a thong attached to a piece of hide on which he sat. The hide was drawn so the hair was next to the snow and it slid along so smooth that we did not mind the load. We took our time and played along near the rear of the caravan. The location of the camping place was on a wooded creek and when we came within sight the leaders were already pitching their lodges. We stood on the edge of the hill overlooking the camp ground and then we followed the trail down the hill. As we were just boys, we had no idea of the weight of our load. As we descended, the load followed so quickly we jumped out of the way. But grandfather slid on down the hill so fast it was no time before he was to the bottom. As he hit the snow-covered sagebrush on the creek bottom, he turned over and over and landed in a heap that looked like a pile of tanned robes. Several women, who were nearby, came running over and helped him up but he was not hurt and joked about the lads giving him a fast ride."

AN OLD MAN, LAST, TOLD THE FOLLOWING STORY:

"A long time ago, when there were no horses, a war party found a lone horse and brought it back with them. The people were amazed to see so large a dog, and they named it Big Dog. And so horses are called today in the Assiniboine language.

"It was so strong that it could carry two men at one time on its back.

"Whenever a war party went forth, they always took the horse with them. On one of those trips an enemy war party was surprised and chased. Someone in the group thought of the idea to carry the slow ones on ahead with the horse. So one rode with him on each trip, and he took enough men to the front so that the enemy was overtaken that way and beaten.

"After that the people worshipped the horse and whenever a war party was to start, the warriors first made sacrifices to it. The war parties were always successful and one time they brought back a large herd of horses. The horses were distributed among the people and, so, for the first time our people owned horses."

An old saying was, "Dogs in the north and horses in the south." This was after our people were in both places.

"A LONG TIME AGO, WHEN THERE WERE NO HORSES, A WAR PARTY FOUND A LONE HORSE ... THE PEOPLE WERE AMAZED TO SEE SO LARGE A DOG. AND SO HORSES ARE BIG DOG IN THE ASSINOBOINE LANGUAGE."

The southern bands were the first to own horses which were captured from enemy tribes to the southwest of them. (In 1754, according to history, Anthony Hendry found horses among the western Assiniboine, probably stolen from the Blackfoot.)

The Plains bands used horses in the chase, so they had their fast buffalo runners and packed the kill on extra horses. The fast horses were never hitched to pull travois or carried packs of any kind.

Although horses were being used by bands south of them, the peoples of the north used dogs for a long time before they finally owned horses. They killed buffaloes by the trap method and usually camped nearby. They used the dogs to move the kill from the trap to the camp.

The bands moved often and when the camp was moved to another location, lodge poles were made into travois. Two poles were sufficient, but in order to haul the extra poles, two or three were used on each side, lashed together. Where dogs were used, only a pair of poles were used for each dog.

A permanent travois was made of two long poles tied together at the small ends with the butt ends spread out; a round or oval-shaped frame was fastened near the middle section. The frame was made of willow bent into shape and the center laced with rawhide strings. The point was padded and placed far up on a horse or dog and held in place by a harness. The poles on a horse travois were crossed and secured with thongs, then padded. The poles on the dog travois were not crossed but came together and bound with wet rawhide which, when dried, held the point strongly together.

Some dogs were in the habit of backing out of their travois, so a belly band was used in addition to the regular breast harness.

Travois horses were ridden by young mothers with their babies and led by women.

When a band was to move to another location, the camp crier, who was instructed by the chief and headmen, made the rounds within the camp circle and proclaimed to the people that the camp would move the next morning. "The grass is getting short; the watering places are becoming stale; wood is scarce and the game is now at a long distance from our camp, so make ready to move tomorrow," sang the crier, repeating the same instructions at intervals until the circle was completed.

When morning came the people watched the emblem that adorned the top of the lodge of the chief. The emblem was usually the tail of a horse or other animal; or an eagle's head, stuffed, and sometimes the tanned skins of different animals. It all depended on what the chief of a band had for his emblem.

When the journey was to be made, the emblem, which was tied to a long lodge pole was taken down. The emblem was pointed in the direction of the new camp location, and the pole was raised on a tripod. If the emblem hung near the ground, that was a sign the journey would be a long one. If the pole was raised so the emblem was high in the air, then only a short move was to be made.

The women, children and old people formed the main caravan. They all traveled afoot except the mothers with newborn babies and those unable to walk. These rode the travois, the travois horses or on extra pack horses. The men walked in groups along the sides, some distance away and others brought up the rear. The chief and the headmen rode horseback far ahead of the movers.

When the new location was reached, the emblem was stuck in the ground in an upright position and the lodges were pitched around it in the form of a circle. The women, with the help of the children, pitched the lodges and attended to the rest of the tasks. The old women got the wood and the young maidens brought water. Young men tarried near the watering places for the chance to court the maidens that came for water. They took the horses to water and remained nearby as an excuse for being there.

The men never helped with the tasks but sat in groups, visiting, until the lodges were all set up.

RIVERS WERE CROSSED IN SKIN BOATS MADE OF BUFFALO HIDES stretched over a circular framework of large willows. It was a basket-like framework with the hide stretched over it. Some were made oblong by sewing together two hides, with the seam through the center. The boats were always laid on the bank, turned over, when not in use.

If a crossing was made in moving to new campgrounds, temporary skin boats were built and taken apart when the crossing had been made.

When a band crossed a large river, like the Missouri, the lodge poles were laced together and another layer laid crossways, then the two layers were made secure with thongs. All the camp equipment was placed on the raft and children and old people rode it. Then several men, all good swimmers, got around and swam across with it. Able-bodied men and women who were poor swimmers were permitted to hang on to the sides and swim along as the raft was towed.

"RIVERS WERE CROSSED IN SKIN BOATS MADE OF BUFFALO HIDES."

During those crossings, the young men vied with one another in skill at swimming. Some swam alongside of their favorite horses while others rode without any kind of a bridle and guided their mounts by patting the necks with their hands. There were daring ones who turned their horses loose and clung to the tails and swam across that way.

Much has been written about the old and feeble being left to die on old camp grounds when a band moved to another place. The well-to-do families, who had the means to move their old relatives, never left any of them to die. It was only those who were poor and could not take their relatives along, who had to do this.

But abandonment was not considered inhuman at that time. It was looked upon as the same as a person dying—nothing could be done about it. The old people understood that, with the infirmities of old age, death was near and so the wish to be left behind came from them.

Usually, as soon as the caravan was out of sight, the aged person committed suicide; the men by knife and the women by hanging themselves to limbs of trees with thongs.

Just before they did away with themselves they sang the death song. Their minds were not on the band that was moving away but on the journey toward the east, to the land of departed relatives. Death in that manner was as honorable as from a coup in battle.

"The old people who were left to die were not many," Mrs. Crazy Bull says. "This act was uncommon. I am now eighty-nine years old and I knew of only one such happening.

"Often times the dogs took after game and the entire load was upset on the prairie ..."

"During the summertime we journeyed about a great deal. It was on one of those moves that a crowd gathered near the edge of a wooded creek. Everyone stopped their travois dogs and horses and went ahead to see what it was about. I was eighteen years old then and was just as curious as the others so I hurried over to the gathering.

"Before I got there, I heard from others on the way that they were looking at the body of an old woman who had been left to die some moons ago. She was of our band and had been left behind but many did not know of it until that day when they saw the dead body.

"Each band usually stopped at the same campgrounds in moving about and we were headed for one of these camps.

"I saw the body hanging to the limb of a tree. It was dried but had not fallen apart and was a ghastly sight. The limbs were hanging straight down like sticks attached to a bundle.

"No one made any attempt to take it down for burial and the band moved on to another camping place.

"The spot, on Little Porcupine Creek, is known to this day as the place where the dried old woman lies."

Courtship and Marriage

A FAIR MAIDEN WAS NOT EASILY COURTED because she was always chaperoned by her grandmother or an older woman who was a relative.

The manner of courtship on the part of a youth was to attract the attention of a maiden by his dress, hunting ability, war record or skill in a game or dance. He did not call on a young woman in her lodge but if he saw her at a gathering, he made it a point to attract her attention in some manner; then they exchanged fond glances. The maiden returned this attention by wearing nice clothes that showed her fine handiwork. Then at the first opportunity the youth approached the girl and they talked together.

Some young men boldly courted while the young woman gathered wood, even though an older woman was near and acted as a chaperon. If a youth's attentions were agreeable to a young woman she carried on a conversation with him, but if she resented them, she ignored him. Sometimes a young man was not so easily driven away and insisted on being heard. In that case the maiden threatened the rash youth with a stick.

It is told that some young men humbled themselves greatly when talking to the maidens they admired. Perhaps they met while the young woman was getting water and the youth may have watched for that chance. The young man's speech would go like this:

"Did you say something? Perhaps I am mistaken. You have been in my thoughts so much and I have imagined many times that you have spoken to me. Now that you are so near, I may seem to hear your voice. If you haven't said anything, it is well and good, for I am like dirt under your feet and why should you waste your kind voice on lowly things. See, I dare not touch you, lest I soil so beautiful a being."

That was a speech of a humble lover. A girl had to show judgment because a desperate lover could resort to "love medicine."

On the other hand there were maidens who went out at night and stood near their lodges to meet their sweethearts. So when the old grandfathers gave advice to their grandsons about love affairs they said, "Do your courting during the day and if you wish to say something to the young woman send a message by your sister or cousin, because maidens who go out after dark to meet young men do not always make good wives."

When parents thought it was time for a son to get married, they asked one of the grandfathers to talk to the young man. The grandmother prepared a dish that the youth was fond of and he was invited over for an evening.

When the meal was finished, the old man slowly filled a pipe, lit it and started to talk. "You are now a man and in a short time you will getting old. Before that time, you must get yourself a woman and live in your own lodge and raise some children.

"Before you do this, first look over the maidens among our people and make up your mind to one. I would advise that you do not pick out one who is too much for looks and has a good figure. Remember, if such a one gains favor in your eyes, she will also attract other men and even though she sits beside you as your woman, men will continue to admire her just the same.

"The relatives of your choice should be looked over to see if her men relations are good providers, skilled hunters, and men who are well known. If her mother is neat and industrious, the daughter will be like her.

"You must turn these things over in your mind many times when some good-to-look-at young woman tries to charm you. You may think you have made a good choice and want to hurry the marriage, but remember to take your time because the one you pick may cause you to live a miserable life.

You may find yourself living in a six-hide lodge (for the poorest people) on the outskirts of an encampment. The clothes you wear may be poorly made and the skins half tanned. Many other things will make your heart heavy.

"The good need not be told. You are grown up; look around and see others. Be like the ones who live in happiness and contentment."

When a young couple decided to marry, the young man brought his wife to the lodge of his folks or he went to live with her people. Then the marriage was announced at the next dance and the relatives gave away presents.

The couple lived with either parents for a year or so. If they lived at the lodge of the wife's parents the son-in-law was expected to supply the meat and do the man's work. The wife did most of the tasks in and about the lodge, if they lived with his folks.

The parents and relatives of a marriageable youth sometimes made a choice for him. Red Feather told the following story:

"My father never talked to me about marriage, but one time, while on a visit to my aunt in another band, she talked right to the point. She always seemed to do the talking for the family. She had a son and daughter. The youth was my age, and we were always together.

"She said, 'You and your cousin (meaning her son) have been visiting back and forth between the two bands and caused us much worry. There is so much danger from war parties traveling about and an enemy could easily waylay and kill you both. You are now grown and should settle down. We have selected a young woman who lives in this band to be your wife. She is strong and well-trained by her mother and no one has, so far, asked for her. We have already arranged everything so you will be married tomorrow.'

"I was not surprised, for I was resigned to the will of my family and my aunt was like my own mother. A man was paid a fee and sent with three horses and some goods to my future wife's folks.

"It was the custom for the bridegroom to paint the face of his bride upon her arrival in the lodge of her future husband, but my cousin said, 'I will relieve you of that task and paint her face myself. Just leave that part to me.'

"The man returned, accompanied by my future wife. She brought food with her, which she placed in front of my aunt. My aunt then seated her beside me and told my cousin to paint her face as he had volunteered to do. My cousin was not so willing to keep his word now that the time had come and said I should paint my own wife's face.

"By that time I thought my heart was going to pound its way out through my breast. I could not move to do anything and my aunt kept repeating that the bride should not be kept waiting. So finally I got up enough courage to perform the rite, and I did not do it so well either. My hands shook so that I just daubed a little paint on each cheek and was finished. After that she accompanied the man back to her home.

"The next day, her folks brought her and two horses, which were loaded with goods to my aunt's lodge. The horses they gave to my uncle and aunt and the goods were bedding and things for us.

"My aunt gave a large feast and the marriage was announced and many things were given away by both parties."

It was customary for older men to bargain for a wife. They gave a fee to a go-between and he made the offer to the girl's parents. If the offer was attractive to the parents, they entreated their daughter to consent to the marriage. The girl could not be compelled to accept but the parents always worked on her affection for her relatives and usually, in the end, there was a marriage.

Some poor parents, or parents who had daughters but no male provider in the family, "gave away" their daughters to prominent men, even though the men already had one or more wives.

There were cases where a child was promised to a grown man, and while the girl was growing up, the prospective husband provided for her and her parents. There were times when a girl, on reaching maturity, refused to fulfill the promise made by her parents.

A man boldly took back his gifts if the girl he bought left his lodge and went back to her folks. Some of these troubles, now and then, had serious consequences and someone was injured or killed.

If a man's wife had more work than she could do in their lodge and had one or more unmarried younger sisters, the man could ask her relatives, through another person for one of them to be his wife. He need not bargain for her as it was considered her duty to her sister to accept and help with the tasks. The parents did not expect anything in return but continued support. Several sisters could marry a man if he was a prominent person, a good provider, and entertained a great deal.

The parents of a boy and the parents of a girl, if the families were close friends, usually planned that the two would marry at maturity. In that case, if some one wanted the girl, she was already promised. And the maidens knew, too, that the young man was as good as married. From childhood, the two were taught to observe the rules that governed a person's behavior and speech when in the presence of a father-in-law or a mother-in-law.

Marriages were dissolved merely by living apart. Sometimes, if the husband was a member of a society, he announced through another that, "He has thrown her away." That was a sign that anyone was free to court the woman. If the man took his wife back, and they lived together as before, it was considered a disgrace. He was dropped from his society and, if he had an office or rank in the organization, it was taken from him and given to someone else.

Children

AN ASSINIBOINE FAMILY WAS SMALL, usually one to three children, born from five to seven years apart.

Babies were brought into the world with the help of two or more old women who made a practice of assisting at births. They were paid a fee, in advance, for their services. If all went well, the women got along all right but sometimes in delayed cases a medicine man was called in to give herbs to the mother. If they did not help he resorted to magic but gave no other assistance. When told that the child had come he smilingly remarked to the nurses, "I told a tortoise to chase the baby out."

As soon as the child was born, one of the women, who had great pride in her good character, took the newborn child, cleaned out its mouth, wrapped it up, and put it in the cradle. By that act the child inherited the good qualities of that woman and of course any bad habits or temper as well. Because of that belief, as soon as a child came, the nurses took stock of themselves and in case none was worthy, they called in some woman with a kind disposition and who was industrious, to act as sponsor. However, in an emer-

"IT WAS GREAT SPORT FOR A GROUP OF BOYS WITH BOWS AND DRIED GRASS ARROWS
TO SURROUND A BATCH OF TALL GRASS AND SHOOT THE MICE..."

gency any of the women served as sponsor regardless of her traits. If that woman was talkative or had a mean temper and, when the child grew up, it had any of those bad qualities, the women said, "See, the sponsor all over again." If it was a good child, the one who sponsored it took great pride in telling others that she was responsible for the good traits of the child.

Oftentimes aunts, although they did not help, waited near at hand to perform the sponsorship act so that the child would be like them. The nurses resented such interference if the aunt's character was not considered to be of the right kind.

Men did not act as sponsors at the birth of children.

The babies were kept in buckskin cradles that re-sembled sleeping bags. The openings, from the top al-most to the bottom, were laced and tied. They were filled with ripe, dried cattails which when fluffed were soft and downy and served as a combina-tion blanket and diaper. The cattails were re-newed as needed.

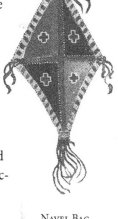

A few days after the birth of a child it was given a common name such as, "The Boy" or, "Good Girl" and it was known by that until the real name was conferred on it at a later ceremony. A child could have several different names; a medicine man's selec-tion, a warrior's, and other common ones. The names could be given in jest or they might be of a descriptive nature.

Navel Bag

When the navel cord was cut off at birth it was placed in a small dia-mond shaped buckskin bag with some tobacco and sewed up. The bag was decorated all over in different designs and beaver claws were sewed to the two side corners and also the bottom point as decorations.

If a medicine man had been called before the birth of a child and had used magic, the navel bag was decorated with a small design representing a tortoise. When children were at play and a design of this kind was noticed on a navel bag, they said to the owner, "Oh, You had to be chased out by an old tortoise."

The little bag was tied high on the back of the child's coat or dress. When tobacco was scarce the bag was taken off and the tobacco emptied. The bag, with the navel cord in it, was packed away in a medicine bundle for a keepsake to be given to the child when it reached maturity.

After the birth of the first grandchild one of the grandmothers gave a feast to announce its arrival. Other children following were not always feasted in this way.

As a part of the ceremony some old woman or old man received a special invitation to the feast and was given a horse or some other large gift. The recipient walked within the camp circle exhibiting the gift and sang a song of thanksgiving and praise.

The next event celebrated by a feast was the child's first birthday, the only birthday in the lifetime of a person that was celebrated. The feast was always sponsored by one of the grandmothers and the grandfather helped in giving personal invitations.

Child's sleeping bag

Some of these birthday feasts were very large when the grandmothers from both sides acted as joint hostesses. The camp crier was given a fee and dispatched to announce the invitation to the people. Everyone was invited to "Come and bring your cup and plate." A medicine man, who was a very close friend of the grandfathers, was asked to serve as master of ceremonies.

When all the people had seated themselves in a circle, an invitation was sent to the mother of the child. Usually the grandmother of the child took the message to her daughter who was waiting in her lodge. The young mother, who knew of the feast beforehand, had the baby dressed in fine clothes.

The baby's sleeping bag, which served as a crib, was elaborately decorated with porcupine quills in many colors and was made for that occasion. If both of the grandmothers were skilled quillworkers, they made the crib together and that was announced at the feast. The grandmothers of the different families tried to outdo each other in making colorful cribs. There was usually much competition in the decoration of the hood and some were so large and decked with so many ornaments that they were cumbersome.

The grandmother proudly carried the child, and the mother followed. The father was already seated with the crowd, and as the feast was sponsored by women, he had no part in it except that he procured the meat used. However, he was just as happy.

At the approach of the women and the child, the master of ceremonies stood up and a hush fell over the crowd. The mother took her seat with the women but the grandmother stood, holding the child just within the circle and in front of the medicine man. The man called on the Great Being to partake of the feast and the pipe offering and to take pity on the two grandmothers who had made the feast-offering to the Being and to the spirits of the departed. He asked that the child might live long and be successful in every walk of life. By his eloquence he held the crowd in a reverent mood, so that at the end of his speech all expressed their approval.

The grandmother then carried the child from one to the other so the people could see it and, as she passed along in the circle, different ones made comments which pleased the sponsors.

Then food was served and, as the feast neared the end, the old men and old women sang songs of thanksgiving. In the songs the names of the child and its grandmothers were praised.

Quite often children were not weaned until their fourth year. It is said that grown children would stop their play and run to their mothers to nurse.

The bringing up of children usually fell to the grandparents even though there was only one child in the family. The parents were always busy with their tasks. The man was often away on hunts, war parties, in other parts of the camp, visiting, or in council, and all of the work about the lodge fell to the young wife. So for that reason the children were left with the old folks.

The grandparents always camped near their son's lodge and if the young wife was an only child her folks were near also. So the children were with their grandparents a good deal of the time. They were delighted to be permitted to stay over night in either one of the old couples' lodges and in that way a deep affection grew up between the young and the old.

Sometimes the old people actually raised grandchildren who were not orphans. Although the children were with their grandparents a great deal their mothers ruled over them in a stern manner. When the boys had passed their tenth birthday it was the fathers and the grandfathers who trained them.

Whenever a father decided that there were to be no more children the last child's hair was tied in a knot on top of its head, a sign to everyone that the child did not have a younger brother or sister. Both boys and girls wore their hair in that style until they grew up when the knot was taken down.

There were many ways for children to enjoy themselves. They played together in large groups until about ten years of age. From then on the boys had their games and, as they grew older, hunted small game.

It was great sport for a group of boys with bows and dried grass arrows to surround a patch of tall grass along the edge of a slough and shoot the mice that ran from one patch to another. Sometimes if the grass was thick and the mice could not be seen, a fire was started. At the approach of the fire the mice ran in all directions.

It is told that on one of these mouse hunts a group of boys let the fire get away and it burned over a large tract of land. The camp soldiers, a group of men who kept order in a band, caught the boys and punished them by destroying their bows and arrows and cutting their clothing into ribbons.

Boys amused themselves in the summer months with a stick game, a mud-throwing game, target shooting, swimming, and dances held in the woods. In more recent years popguns were made from ash wood and loaded with wood pulp and used in mimic wars.

The girls during the summer months played camp with toy lodges made out of large cottonwood leaves. These were pitched in groups to represent bands and visits were made from one group to another. This game was kept up until the people moved to another place; then the girls would again start new villages.

In winter, tops made from buffalo horns or ash wood were spun on the ice. Sticks were thrown at targets placed against snow banks. The horns of yearling buffaloes, attached to long sticks, were thrown and slid on the ice.

Sliding down hills was the most popular sport in which the boys and girls mingled in the afternoons. They used pieces of hides or dried badger skins for sleds.

During the long evenings boys and girls were almost always in their lodges. Often they listened to mythical tales told by their grandparents. Sometimes a mother prepared some food and invited the neighboring children and an old man, who was a good story teller, to entertain them for an evening.

The small ankle-bones of the buffalo tied to the middle of a sinew ring and spun, provided an evening's amusement in winter.

The old men, when too old to join in the hunt, made bows and arrows for their grandsons and taught them the use of weapons. As the old men had much time, they took great pains to teach and to train the children. They spoke words of advice to them in a way that made them realize the important place they would have in life if they obeyed. Always they looked to the future life of the child, so that he would become a good hunter and a great warrior.

The boys at an early age took their grandfathers' advice seriously. They matured early and were eager to try out the things their advisers talked about.

Some fathers shamed grown sons, when they had slept late, by saying, "How can you join a war party if you love your sleep so much. By this time of the day the party will be far away, and you will be left behind." Water was thrown on boys to waken them if they were late sleepers.

A man named Last tells the story about an unusually harsh father:

"Skin Cap had two sons whom he trained to be warriors. The man was very rough with his boys. Oftentimes he dragged them out of bed and ducked them in the creek in the very early morning. When they were very young he placed them on fast buffalo runners, and urged the horses to a fast pace by riding just behind them.

"One of the boys was born a cripple and died young, but the other one grew up and was a fearless warrior.

"Skin Cap was looked upon by the people as a cruel father and to this day, we who knew him, remember him by his harsh methods of training his two sons."

As a rule children of the Assiniboine were never whipped or handled roughly. Skin Cap's method of training was an exception. If grown boys did things contrary to their fathers' wishes they were talked to and made to realize their mistakes. If a lad was listless and easy going, his father spoke to him in the following manner. "Among our people everyone is expected to marry and raise children. In order to make a success of marriage the father must be a good provider and that means a good hunter. It is time that you think of these things. Look to your equipment and also learn to use it skillfully. Study the habits of animals and birds and learn to take them at the right time and in the correct manner. Make your kills neatly and quickly or else you and your family will have to eat sour meat from exhausted game.

"If you do not learn to judge good buffalo meat on the hoof during a chase, you may take one that will make a laughingstock of you and the hunters will always remind you of it at gatherings.

"Learn to butcher without help and to tie the parts together so that they will hang properly on your pack animal.

"If you do not pay any attention to these things before you marry, how are you going to feed your wife and children? You may never get a woman to sit beside you if she knows of your helplessness. The women will find you out, pass the word among their kind and will say, 'Whoever wants to live on the outskirts of an encampment will marry that lazy fellow.'

"Before you get married join at least one war party so that you can tell of it whenever the occasion arises. If you do not possess one good war exploit you will be embarrassed at a feast when the host sets special food apart for those who first can recount a deed and are then able to partake of the food."

The fathers cautioned their boys, "Don't take anything that does not belong to you. If you wish for anything, ask for it, or get the owner's permission to use it. Don't go prowling about at night, you may run into danger or you may be blamed for something which you perhaps did not do."

The grandfathers were soft-spoken to the boys. The old and the young became close friends and on that account the boys were often with the grandfathers. The advice given was simple and kindly, "If you see an old man doing something and he seems to need help, don't hesitate to offer assistance. If a blind old man is feeling his way with his cane, go to him and say, 'Grandfather, let me lead you where you wish to go,' and then take hold of his stick and lead him along, on smooth paths, to his destination. That old man may impart a word of advice to you that may make you a great man some day. In this day of so much danger, a man does not know how long he is going to live. So when a man reaches the age of gray hairs, it is because he is wise, and therefore, he can pass the secret of his long life to some good boy who does him a kindness."

GIRLS WERE WATCHED AND TRAINED MORE THAN THEY WERE TALKED TO. Wherever they wished to go, the grandmothers accompanied them and because they were chaperoned from birth, they seemed to expect their grandmothers or aunts to go with them.

The mothers spoke to their daughters, "Don't rummage through bags that belong to others for if you do, warts will grow on your hands. Repeated acts will make the warts grow larger and, in time, they will cover your hands.

"When company comes to our lodge, play outside and don't listen to grown-ups when they are talking as you may thoughtlessly repeat some bit of gossip and cause trouble between families."

Children were taught to address their parents as father or mother and their grandparents as grandfather or grandmother. Mention of the names of other relatives had to be preceded by the relationship, as. "My uncle, Red Feather," "My aunt, Wing Woman," "Cousin, Scalps Them."

As all old people were called grandparents, children addressed those other than their own grandfolks, as, "Grandfather White Shield" or "Grandmother Calf Woman."

The parents' and grandparents' love for their children and grandchildren was shown in many ways. They celebrated with a feast at the birth of a child and again when it was named; the first birthday; the first small game killed by a boy; the first handicraft of a girl; the first time either boy or girl joined in a dance. It was only the first of any event in the lives of children that was celebrated. If parents could not afford a feast, they gave away things but only to the old.

THE LOVE AND FONDNESS THAT PARENTS AND GRANDPARENTS HAD for their children is shown in the following story told by Wing Woman:

"My brother, who was seven years older than I, was kicked by a horse. The injury was near the temple and, although he seemed to be on the way to recovery, he died very suddenly. My parents were grief-stricken and refused to have the boy buried.

"The body was lashed to a travois and as it was in the late summer, it was not long before the body decomposed. From time to time, the coverings were changed and flies were kept away with a smudge. When camp was moved to another location, the burial travois was drawn by a gentle horse that did not mind his strange burden. As a rule, horses were afraid of dead bodies.

"In time the body dried up and became a light bundle so that when a new camping place was reached and while the women were busy setting up the lodges, the horse grazed about until the travois was removed.

"The body was never taken off the travois, which was always leaned against the outside of our lodge at the back and my father slept in the part of the lodge nearest to it.

"During the late fall, a group of prominent men of our band came to our lodge with my uncle as spokesman and besought my parents to consent to the burial of the body. My father could not refuse, because they brought a peace pipe with them which was lit. My father was asked to smoke it and when he did so, they knew their mission was accomplished. So, at last the body was buried."

An old man named Bad Hawk told this story:

"My grandfather, Spotted Beaver, was a well-known medicine man of the magic clan. He had an only daughter who died at the age of twelve years. Day after day, he went to her burial place to be near her. As he was a magic man, he believed in things supernatural and took comfort in the thought that his daughter's spirit was near and heard his voice.

"When the body had decayed and dried, my grandfather took the bones from the limbs and cut them in length about one and one-half inches, cleaned and smoothed out the cores and laced them on a buckskin string.

"That weird necklace was always worn by my grandfather. When he took part in different medicine dances and gatherings, where the performers stripped down to their clouts and moccasins, he never took the necklace off but wore that string of bones as a part of his magic and relied on the spirit of his daughter for guidance."

Crazy Dog Stories

MAD WOLVES AND COYOTES WERE KNOWN TO EXIST in the land of the Assiniboine at one time.

They did not run in packs but were always alone. They were called *Sunk-Naskinyan*, which meant crazy dog.

The animals were in a scabby condition, without hair, and their tails appeared shorter than the regular wolf or coyote tail due to loss of hair. They traveled about running in circles, biting their flanks and now and then their tails.

The people were afraid of them because a bitten person, even a travois dog, became mad and acted like them.

When the animals saw people, they ran in that circling fashion toward them. They were known to come into an encampment during the night and, when one came, all the travois dogs in the camp would be out after it. Oftentimes dogs were bitten. They were quickly put to death and afterwards burned.

Children who did not mind were told by their mothers or grandmothers, "If you don't keep quiet and go to sleep the crazy dog will come and bite you, then you will be crazy too." Sometimes they said, "Listen ! I hear a crazy dog barking and if it hears you, it will surely come."

The old man named Duck told this story:

"When I was about fourteen years old, I accompanied my father to where he killed and left two buffaloes. The time of the year was in the Long Day Moon (February). Because it was far from our camp, we took several horses to pack the meat back.

"On the way over, we saw a coyote at a long distance, traveling in a zigzag fashion; it went in one direction and then changed its course to another. My father knew what it was but did not seem to notice it for sometime. Finally he said, 'What you see over there is a crazy dog. When it sees us, it will come this way and when close enough I will kill it.'

"I had heard of the crazy dogs but had never seen one. It was told that, when one came to a camp everybody ran into their lodges and made the door flaps secure from within. The camp dogs would bark and go after the crazy one, which fought them back. The men watched from within the lodges and, when they had a chance, killed the mad one with arrows. The arrows used and the dead crazy dog were then burned together.

"The animal came closer and closer toward us as father had foretold. We moved slowly along and finally stopped near the edge of a cut bank.

"When the mad one was a short distance away, my father got off his horse and handed the rope to me. While I held all horses, he walked over to the edge of the steep bank. There he stood waiting, as the coyote was headed toward us from that direction and would have to climb over the bank to get to us.

"When it got closer, I had a good look at the strange animal. As it came, it circled around and around, biting its flank and tail; then it would reverse and go through the same motion. In that way it took some time to cover the distance to where we waited.

"Imagine my fear at the sight of a real crazy dog; the kind that, even the mention of it, made us children behave; here it was coming toward me. But, between it and I, stood my father which, no doubt, was what kept me from fleeing.

"Afterward, when I thought of it, the coyote was, perhaps, in distress and was coming to us for help. Like we say 'It ran to us for pity.' The eyes were wild-looking, bulged out and shiny, not seeming to be looking at any one thing.

"When it came against the bank, my father leaned over and killed it. I jumped off my horse and ran over where father already stood looking at it. The hair was nearly all gone off its body, except on the legs and feet. The tail looked short without the long hair that usually made the tails on coyotes so bushy and long.

"My father said, 'Take a good look at this thing, it is not often that a person sees one of these so close. They are dangerous and if one should bite a person, one of our dogs, or even one of its own kind, that bitten one would become crazy.

"So, the crazy dogs are real after all and not like the mythical giant, who carried a large bag on its back; the large one was supposed to wander about the camp after dark, listening at every lodge for some child who was not in bed and quiet. If he heard one who did not mind its parents, he removed a bottom peg on the lodge, reached in and snatched that child away. When all the children were quiet, he feasted on the ones he collected in his bag. That and the crazy dog made us children behave; one an imaginary being and the others real live animals.

"No one in my time, that I knew of, had been bitten by a crazy dog, but there is an old story about a man who was bitten by one:

THE VICTIM OF A CRAZY DOG BITE, WRAPPED IN A BUFFALO HIDE,
WAS HELD OVER THE FIRE.

"One winter, long ago, a man was out hunting; when he came back he told his wife that he felt queer all over. He told several, who came to see him, that a hairless wolf bumped against him and after that he felt that way. They said, 'A crazy dog has bitten you and we must call a medicine man, one who is skilled in the treatment of that kind; fill a medicine pipe at once; gather together things for sacrifices and take them to him.'

"When the medicine man came, he ordered a long fire built; one that would be two camp fires to burn side by side. He asked for an untanned buffalo hide, with the hair removed. The sick man was laid on the hide and rolled in. The ends were secured with thongs and, when finished, he lay as if in a long bag.

"The medicine man prayed aloud to his Being, after which he gave instructions to some men. While several singers beat on small round hide drums and sang songs the medicine man selected, the men, two on each end, held the bundle over the fire. They turned it slowly over and over above it.

"They went through that motion four times, while the medicine man stood near by directing the whole affair.

"When they unwrapped the sick man, he was covered with perspiration and also a heavy covering of gray hair which resembled the hair on a wolf. As he was being rubbed dry, the hair also came off so that his skin was as before. When all was over, the hide with the hair and all other things used were burned.

"The man was cured but the people changed his name, so that he was known thereafter as Hair Man."

War Parties

THE PRINCIPAL AMBITION OF ALL MEN was to join war parties. To a warrior's name was added the comment, "He joined many different war parties," which meant that he was a brave man and others knew it. To be possessed of only one war achievement was enough to be admitted into a guest lodge where a feast was prepared for men who could, if called upon, relate a war deed.

At gatherings men were called upon to act as masters of ceremonies. In order to fill that position, they first had to give an account of some exploit. Warriors were especially invited to a feast to name a child. They were given a fee, as well as the honor of naming the child.

A warrior's stories never became old or worn out by being retold at dances. The stories of war achievements were good until the death of the person. If

"PRINCIPAL AMBITION OF ALL MEN WAS TO JOIN WAR PARTIES … IT WAS IMPORTANT
THAT BOYS BE TRAINED EARLY IN LIFE TO BECOME WARRIORS."

a story of one of his deeds was given to a younger person, that story could be retold again and again, even though the real owner was dead.

For these reasons and many others it was important that the boys be trained early in life to become warriors. As the boys grew older, the grandfathers shifted from mythical tales to real war stories. Accounts of different persons who were known to the story teller and to the boys interested them. In that way interest and a desire to accompany a war party was aroused in the youths.

The old men said to the youths, "The man who stays home and courts women will some day find himself old and the women will not want him any more. That man is just as well-off dead for his life is wasted. But the man with a good war record, if he reaches gray hairs, can still tell his stories to his grandchildren and those children will be proud of their grandfather. So, while you are young and before you have a woman, join a war party to make a name for yourself. Even though you may lie dead in the enemy country and make green grass, your name will always be mentioned when that part of the country is talked about."

The men who headed war parties were not the medicine men who treated the sick or took charge of ceremonial dances. They were leaders who were instructed by different Beings in visions or dreams. When a leader-to-be had fasted for several days, alone and away from camp, he was shown a vision of a journey into an enemy's country where he was promised horses and scalps, perhaps other deeds as well. He was also instructed to make a medicine garment. It could be a cap, coat or the skin of some animal used as a scarf. The Being who gave the instructions were always copied. For example, if the Being was the Sacred Wolf, the cap would be made of wolf skin or the whole skin be used as a scarf. Such garments were worn only during the final march into camp or battle. Otherwise, they were folded and made into a bundle which was packed at the side or carried on the back. It was called a sacred bundle.

Young men who joined war parties borrowed sacred bundles from their fathers, grandfathers or other relatives who had them and who stayed at home. Those young men received the necessary instructions in the care and use of the bundles from the owners. Some owners had the right to make bundles and made similar ones for the young men, sometimes for a fee.

MAKING MEDICINE FOR A WAR PARTY.

When a war leader had a suitable vision, he called a number of able warriors to his lodge and told them of his intentions. It was an honor to be invited by an experienced leader to join a war party. The number was never large. Twelve was the average number that formed a party. When a trip was planned it was kept secret and when all preparations for it were completed, the group started out during the night. That was done so that only the ones invited would be in the party. However, many times after marching a day or two one or more men from home overtook the party. They were always allowed to join the group.

Almost always the men started out on foot with the prospect of riding back. Each man carried a pack, containing needed articles.

On long trips an extra bow was taken along. Moccasins were most important so several pairs were taken along. They traveled during the day and when near the border of their country, game was taken and much cooked meat was packed in their bags. Fires were not built when in the enemy country.

A war party traveled single file, summer or winter. The war leader always took the lead. The "first timers" or young men on their first war journey were in the rear. When the leader stopped, everyone did the same. Whatever he said was passed back from one to the other. When pursued, they either spread out and ran in line, or ran in all directions, everyone for himself.

Before leaving his own country, the leader unpacked his sacred bundle and spread it out before him. He sang and went through his ritual and make a sacrifice to his Being. He prayed that some knowledge of the enemy might be shown him. The men all helped towards the sacrifice. As each member deposited his offering before or on top of the leader's sacred bundle, he prayed for horses, scalps or a count in a coup, which was achieved by killing or capturing either a man or woman in an enemy tribe, stealing horses, or some other brave deed.

Usually the leader told of a vision and gave some information of what possibly would happen. He gave advice to the members as to the manner in which they should approach the camp or the enemy.

The party stayed together from the start even during an open attack on the enemy. If a member was wounded the person who rescued him counted it a war deed. If a person brought back the dead body of a member, unscalped, at the risk of his life, that also counted. Sometimes, when the party retreated and was hard pressed, a member stood the enemy off until the others got away. Many times, that one gave his life so that the others could reach safety. If he came back wounded, he was eligible to close a dance. When a dance was nearly over, a warrior, who had been wounded in battle, was asked to re-enact the manner in which he had been wounded. Then at the conclusion of his act, he led the way out of the dance lodge and the crowd followed, thus ending the affair.

When a war party raided a camp to take horses, everyone had to look out for himself. The group agreed to meet at a certain place and, if all went well, they gathered there to plan the return home. But if the enemy found out about the raid, then each one pursued the best course he knew. Unreliable members made straight for home when they were satisfied with the number of horses they had taken. That was one of the reasons why leaders took pains to select men who could be trusted. If one or more did not return to the spot agreed on, then the members knew those either had been killed or that they were hiding and would catch up with the party later. But if the reputations of the missing ones were questionable, then there was only one thought, "They have gone home."

When the war party arrived within sight of their home camp, they attracted the attention of the people by an appropriate sign. If the party had been successful, a member ran in a zigzag fashion. Then the people went to them and took the scalps, horses or other objects that they had captured. A short dance followed in which the people held up the objects. Everyone was happy. After that the owners gave these things away to the ones whom they had in mind. A son-in-law usually brought a scalp and presented it to his mother-in-law through a third party. Some gave scalps directly to their fathers-in-law.

If the war party lost one or more members, they first attracted the people's attention, and then threw a robe, rolled into a ball-like shape, high in the air. The number of members slain was shown by the number of times the robe was thrown. A delegation was sent to meet the party and obtain the names of the ones killed. The party was then escorted back to camp and word was taken to the relatives of those slain.

However, this custom was not always observed. Some warriors surprised the home folks by an unheralded parade around the inside of the camp circle with horses that they had brought back, after which all held a war dance.

WHEN AN ENEMY WAS KILLED only four persons could count coup. The first to touch him with any object, counted it as the coup and those who followed counted it as the second, third and fourth coups. The first coup was considered a higher honor than the shot that killed an enemy from a distance.

Sometimes an enemy feigned death and drew an ambitious warrior within range of his weapon with fatal results. For that reason, to count the first coup a person risked his life more than the one who shot from a distance. A person was allowed to kill and then take the first coup as well.

The first one who took a scalp kept it, but if any small patches of hair were left on the head, and another took them, that person was also eligible to join in a scalp dance.

The first one who sank a tomahawk into a scalped head, counted that as a war deed. It was considered a minor act.

An eagle tailfeather, dyed red and worn upright at the back of the head during a dance, indicated that the wearer had killed an enemy. For as many as he had slain he added as many dyed feathers. They were not worn as a headdress but merely stuck separately in the hair. When a warrior killed a woman who belong to an enemy tribe, two gull feathers from the ring-billed gull were worn in the hair. And if he already wore one or more red feathers, he added the gull feathers to them.

When tips of coyote tails were worn they were sewed to the heels of moccasins. Leggings, below the knees, were painted with pictures of hoofprints; these indicated that the person had taken horses in the summer season. If he brought back horses during the winter he wore white weasel skins among the fringes of his coat sleeves.

If a warrior struck the lodge of an enemy with any object held in one hand, it was an honor and that person could re-enact it at a dance during a parade. If one shot at lodges from a distance, that also counted and could be re-enacted.

The horses picketed to the lodges were usually the pet runners of any tribe. It was an act of bravery to cut the rope and steal such horses, although stealing of any horse was a brave deed.

THE OLD MAN NAMED DUCK TOLD THIS STORY ABOUT WAR:

"My first war experience was not on one of those journeys into the enemy country. It was in a chase after several Nez Perce men who were near our camp, but that is another story.

"My first war party trip was headed by White Dog, a noted medicine-man warrior. There were nineteen in the party and another youth and myself were the two first-timers. It was in the summer and we headed for Piegan country.

"The first-timers usually attended to the chores about the camp when a stop was made. The lad who waited on the leader made things comfortable for him, cooked choice meat cuts and placed them before him at meal time, and sometimes packed his belongings. This was all done so that the leader might be pleased and perhaps return the favor.

"When a leader or any of the older men, who had made many successful war trips, was pleased with the attentions shown them by the first-timers, he stepped aside many times so that the youths could count coup. Or, when horses were taken, the youths were given the chance to take one or more for themselves. When the lads were left at the camp while a horse raid was in progress, they were given their share as though they had been in the raid. Many times the older men told the lads to take their choice of horses. So it paid to be industrious and to respect the older and more experienced ones who were responsible for the success of a war party.

"We journeyed leisurely while we were still in our own country but when we entered the enemy country of the Piegans we traveled by night.

"One morning while looking for a suitable day camp, we scattered to look for water. The lad and myself were together and fortunately we found water right away. We filled our water bags which were made from buffalo stomachs. As I closed the opening with the draw string, I saw a rider who had just topped a ridge. We were already down on our knees among clusters of young pine, so we could not be seen very easily.

"We put the water bags on our backs and crawled behind a larger bush. From there we watched and saw three more riders join the first. They surveyed the country to our right. They seemed satisfied with their view of the country, and all rode away. By their actions, we were positive that they had not seen us.

"We hurried back to our camp and when we knew we could be heard by our party, gave the cry, a straight call that resembled a high-pitched howl. It was a cry that meant an enemy was seen by a scout.

"When we arrived among our men, the leader filled the medicine pipe. It had a black stone bowl with a plain ash stem and was always carried by leaders to be used when offerings were made. He lit it and took a few puffs after which he extended it, stem foremost, and each of us took a draw.

"When the medicine pipe was thus offered to a scout, the information that he brought must be the truth and a fact and not any hurried observation or guess work.

"After we had taken several quick puffs from the pipe, the leader said, 'Speak up, young men, and tell your story.'

"So that was an achievement for both of us 'to see the enemy without being seen.' We could re-enact the scene at home during a dance or at a gathering. Each of us already had a story.

"MY FIRST WAR PARTY TRIP ... INTO THE PIEGAN COUNTRY ... WAS HEADED BY
WHITE DOG, A NOTED MEDICINE-MAN WARRIOR."

Two scouts were sent to locate the camp and by evening they were heard by their call, the short bark of the coyote. 'They have seen an encampment,' they all said.

"They reported a very large band camped in a valley, and, during the afternoon, another band came and camped with them. So we marched during the night and reached the edge of the camp.

"The scouts said that there was a celebration of some kind and many horsemen were in a parade within the camp circle.

"It was still early, for many lodges were lit up and the singing of songs came forth from some of them, no doubt the after effects of the celebration.

"The leader and his brother said, 'We will go into camp to see how things are. If we have a chance, we will bring horses here. Wait for us.'

"We waited for some time and then there were whispers of discontent among the party. A large group headed by Wets It, left us and also went to the camp. By that time, I was uneasy and said, 'I have come a long way for a chance like this.' And with that, I left them.

"I heard footsteps behind me and soon two more caught up to me. The three of us entered the encampment. We separated with the understanding that we would meet later where the others still waited.

"I came to a large lodge where a number of horses were picketed close by. I crouched down and looked them over against the horizon. 'They were not all tied and I threw a loop and caught one, which came to me. I caught one more by the loop and took three of the picketed ones. By now I had five head which I led away a short distance and mounted the first one I had caught. That horse was a gray, a very fat animal. Its mane and tail were cut short which showed that the animal was made to mourn for his deceased master. There were still decorations and paint on the horse from the mourning parade.

"I returned to the others and soon my two partners came back with more horses. We gave a mount to each of the three who were waiting. At that moment we heard a shot on the other side of the camp circle. Several more shots were fired and then there was commotion in the Piegan camp.

"Before we decided on any plan of escape, there was a rumbling noise, made by many riders. They went in the direction from which we came but more and more were heard galloping about the camp.

"We fled in the opposite direction and climbed the side of a mountain.

We hid the horses in a deep ravine and climbed to the peak of the mountain where we hid among the rocks.

"By that time it was daylight and from our position we saw a sight that gave us a chill.

"The whole camp was alive with people and horses. In the direction from which we had come there was a cloud of dust kicked up by the pursuers. More riders rode around inside of the camp circle.

"Someone said, 'Let us get out of sight as some object may be accidentally reflected in the sun and they will notice and make a search here.' We crawled far back under the protruding rocks and slept there the rest of the day. When night came we took the horses. Then we circled wide around the encampment and headed towards home.

"By mere accident, we found another group that also escaped notice by the enemy. My young friend was in that group and he, too, had captured a horse.

"The leader of the war party and his brother had hidden the same as we with a large band of horses far beyond our hiding place. They came home with their horses several days after we did.

"The whole band of mounted pursuers had found the trail of Wets It's group, who entered the camp behind the leader and his brother. Although they did not recapture their horses, they killed one member of that group.

"Sometimes, in the excitement, the most experienced men made mistakes. The group that was overtaken did not scatter out as they should and the result was that they left a trail very easily followed by the enemy.

"For me that trip turned out to be a horse raid. I did not fire a shot," Duck said.

Dances and Social Gatherings

WHEN PEACE WAS MADE WITH NEARBY TRIBES and warfare was being brought to an end, the people devoted more time to social dances and gatherings. Women and children who never joined with the men except at the return of war parties or in religious ceremonies, now had their parts in dances and other social activities.

When the fall social functions in a band were to begin, the chief called a council of all the headmen to the guest lodge. After all had come, the chief, who was seated in the back of the lodge which was the place of honor, asked the two servers to pass the food around.

As the men ate they talked about different happenings among the people. Some told hunting stories and others told amusing jokes played on their brothers-in-law. Those that wished a second cup of beverage left their cups upright while the ones who had finished turned them over with the bottoms up. In that way the servers did not disturb a person who was telling a story.

THE GRASS DANCE
"WHEN PEACE WAS MADE WITH NEARBY TRIBES AND WARFARE WAS BEING BROUGHT TO AN END, THE PEOPLE DEVOTED MORE TIME TO DANCES ..."

When the food was eaten, the chief slowly filled the ceremonial pipe. One of the servers took a live coal from the fire and placed it on the tobacco in the pipe bowl. The chief gave a few puffs and, pointing with the mouthpiece foremost toward the sky, offered it to the Thunder Bird, who represented the birds that flew through the air. Then he pointed the stem down toward the ground and offered it to the earth which produced all things— even things that the Thunder Bird could kill and take.

When the pipe offering was done the chief passed the pipe to the one at his left, as it must go in the same direction that the sun travels on its journey.

There was silence as the chief leaned back against the only decorated willow back rest in the lodge. He now spoke, "The crier has invited you to come. You are all here. You have eaten and will now smoke. The buffalo has been taken, much cured meat and other foods are stored away by the women, soon the different dances and gatherings will start. The ones who are at the head of the dance circle have served for a long time and they are tired. It is now time that we all talk here. New names will be mentioned of ones who will lead in the dances. While the pipe is passed around let us meditate in a careful way so that the names we select will be ones who will fill the positions well and make the hearts of our people glad."

If the old leadership was made up of older people and the council wished the affairs to be more interesting, they selected children from prominent families to be leaders of the different groups that made up the dance circle. In order that the ones selected would be sure to serve, the names of favorite children in well-to-do families were placed on the list. When all positions were filled the meeting was ended.

No one was told of the names selected and nothing more was done until the first big gathering. Everyone knew that at that time the old leaders would retire and new ones would take their places, so everyone attended.

The dance started out in the ordinary way with the old leaders in their accustomed places. When the main parts of the dance were over the announcer made a speech in which he told the people that it was now time to name new leaders and he also thanked the retiring ones for their management during their time.

Because the principal dance, where the whole tribe took part, was the time to make known the new group, a brave heart song was sung by the regular singers. The old leaders, with their officers, danced in groups and when all groups stood side by side they formed a circle. Only the leaders and officers were eligible in the circle, but if relatives wished to make donations in honor of any of them, they also danced in the groups where their relatives took part.

When the song ended the first retiring leader stepped forward into the center accompanied by the announcer. He whispered his speech to the announcer who proclaimed it to the people, after which the leader and his relatives gave away many things. Sometimes horses were led into the dance circle and given away, usually to someone who was in need of a horse. The other leaders of groups and officers followed likewise until all of them were heard and then all took their seats.

The announcer came forward and now told the audience what the council had proposed. As he announced the name of the first child to be the leader, he walked about in the center and voiced approval of the selection. He began to sing a brave heart song; at the same time the singers beat gently on the drum and started the song of leadership, placing the name of the child in the wording of the song. The announcer's voice was somewhat drowned by the drum and singers but he kept on, accompanied by a lot of old men and women.

With all the singing of brave heart songs, sung by different groups, only a heart of stone would refuse the position offered. The father holding the hand of his child, with the mother just behind, came dancing toward the center of the circle, amid renewed songs from the audience, while the regular singers continued their song to which the new leader and the parents kept time. Soon relatives of the chosen joined them, each dancing behind the other in single file.

The song ended and the other names were announced. A new song, with appropriate wording was sung for each new leader of a group. With all the relatives and the close friends of the parents of the chosen children, the dance circle became very large. As each father proclaimed through the announcer that his child was honored and would support the social circle, a different song was started up. The old leaders joined the new ones and both parties danced together. Later on in the dance, all the dancers joined in and even the spectators rose up and either stood or danced in their places. Then the affair ends.

The different positions given to the children were the heads of groups that made up the dance circle. The leadership over all the dance groups, which was called *Waci-in-tancan* or Dance Leader, was the highest position and also the most costly. Only a member from the best family was given that honor. Because the holder was expected to be generous and shoulder the main part of the upkeep of the dance circle, there were some who declined the position when it was offered to them. But if the favorite child in a well-to-do family was chosen the parents could not refuse; for to decline was an act that caused much camp talk. "Have you heard", they would say, "that he has turned aside the position offered his child? His wife, too, agrees with him. They must love their horses and goods much more than their child. Goods become old and worn, horses become useless in a short time, but the good acts done for the love of children become stories good for the ears of people from other bands; they become as coveted things and are placed side by side with the stories of war achievements."

THE STATIONS OF THE REST OF THE LEADERS were on an even footing and so each group always tried to outdo the other in dress, amount of food taken to the dance, donations to old people, entertaining visitors from other bands, and in many other ways tried to draw the attention and praise of the people toward their group. This made the gatherings successful. In order that all the leaders and officers would surely be present at a gathering, the camp crier, who was responsible for that, visited the lodge of each one and took away an object that was much thought of by the owner. When the owners attended they received their projects back. The articles of those not present, when the crier first announced the names of the owners, were destroyed in full view of the audience as a warning. It was known that the crier once took a child leader to the dance site and forced the attendance of the parents and relatives.

The children who headed social groups were dressed in very elaborate costumes. As the leaders were from families who could afford such costumes, the relatives usually worked with the parents and made a full dress for their boy or girl when the child was made leader of a group.

The boy leader of the entire dance circle, called the *Waci-in-tancan* (pronounced, Wa-Chee-Inton-Chon), was dressed in a complete buckskin outfit. The shirt, leggings and moccasins were beaded or decorated with quill work of uniform design. A small war bonnet of eagle tailfeathers was worn.

Sometimes a row of the same kind of feathers, made into a tailpiece that reached to the ground, was attached to the back of the bonnet. In his left hand he carried a coup stick wrapped with quill work, or some other object suitable to his position. His face was painted all over with light yellow- or red-earth paint and over it small dots or lines were put on with a paint of different color. The boy always headed the male dancers and when his special song was sung, he danced alone through the first song period.

Then the drummers increased their beats, which was a signal for the entire male group to "help their little leader." They danced around him and after a time he led the group, and the rest followed single file once around the circle to their seats. Because the boy was trained to follow the song, which was arranged to govern the performance, he acted his part to perfection.

A girl was placed at the head of the part performed by the women. That position was called *Wabaha-Yuha, Wabaha-Uha* which meant Staff Bearer. Her dress was of tanned antelope skin decorated with porcupine quills in many colors. The sleeves were made extra long and then fringed up to just below the elbows, so that the long strings hung gracefully. The bottom of the dress, which came part way below the knees, was edged with the shells of deer hoofs. A wide beaded belt, with a long extension that hung in front reaching nearly to the ground, was worn. The designs on her leggings and moccasins were the same as those on the dress so that her complete attire was a matched outfit. Her hair, parted in the middle, was braided loosely in two braids that hung down over her breast and several strands of small colored beads were tied to the tips. A little vermillion-colored paint was put on each cheek and that was rubbed down so that it shown faintly. She wore no ornaments on her head except a single downy white eagle feather which was tied at the back.

If she was able, she carried the regulation staff. This was a round stick about seven feet long, wrapped the full length with strips of tanned otter skin. Two or more eagle feathers were tied at the top. The bottom end was sharpened so that when the women were seated it was stuck upright in the ground in front of their group. The staff, which represented leadership, was handed down from time unknown.

The staff was once carried only by the leader of the No Flight dance, men's society. When a group, made up of members of the No Flight society, went on a war journey the leader carried the staff which he used as a spear. Many stories are told of the leaders who showed much bravery, with the use of the staff as a weapon.

In late years, when the men and women joined together in dances, it was told that one time when the No Flights were dancing with the leader in their midst, the wife of the leader boldly came forward and danced beside her husband. After the dance she proclaimed through the announcer that her husband, who was very dear to her, looked tired and so she helped him dance. From that time on the women were allowed to dance the No Flight dance alongside of their husbands.

Later the woman who headed the women's circle dance was allowed to carry the staff. But two members from the society, who had war records, always joined the women dancers and danced just ahead of the woman leader, "to pave a path for the woman who carried their staff." This honor was later conferred on the children.

PART III

LODGES, FOOD AND GAMES

Buffalo—Staff of Life

Fire Making

Foods

The Old Woman Who Tricked Her Captors

Lodges, Clothing and Ornaments

Stone and Bone Articles

Games

Buffalo —Staff of Life

To the Assiniboine, the buffalo was more than an animal. It was the staff of life. No other animal gave so much to the people as that great shaggy creature. For that reason, the buffalo was studied more closely than any other animal.

Its name was given to children so they would be hardy and reach maturity quickly; organizations were named after it; medicine men relied on the powers of the Spirit Buffalo to help them perform their rituals more successfully. A chief had the long forelock of a bull tied to the tip of a lodge pole and had it placed among the rest of the poles of his lodge, as an emblem. The head was placed on the ground, outside, and close to the back of the lodge with offerings laid on top of it.

To an unobservant person, all buffaloes in a herd looked alike. Only the usual kinds that made up the herd, such as the bulls, cows, heifers, young bulls and the general run of the calves, were noticeable. But not so with the Assiniboine. To them there were many kinds and sizes of buffaloes in a herd and much to know about them.

"To an unobservant person, all buffaloes in a herd looked alike ...
not so with the Assiniboine ... there were many kinds and sizes in a
herd and much to know about them."

Mating time was in Red Berries moon (July). The bulls, grouped in small and large herds, roamed peacefully by themselves. But after they joined the cows the bull buffaloes became mean and vicious both toward each other and any Indians who approached them.

Whenever two bulls fought each other the main herd circled around them. Other bulls in the herd would be pawing dirt and bellowing deep down in their throats while the cows looked on. The battle was always to the death of one of the warriors. They fought forehead to forehead, pushing each other backwards. If one gave up and turned or tried to jump out of the way, he was gored in the flank. One swift move forward and a quick turn of the head made a long and deep gash in the flank. The intestines immediately came out, resulting in death. The victor never paid any attention to the victim after the fatal hook was made.

It is told that during a fight the bulls paid no attention to persons. Although the main herd fled at the approach of a mounted person, the pair fought on so that many times Assiniboine onlookers saw at close range the outcome of such encounters.

Oddly, old bulls mated with young cows and young bulls with the matured cows. Early in the mating season, perhaps to avoid fighting, a bull with one or more cows would stay in deep coulees, quite a distance from large herds. That was a common sight and when a group was seen the following remark was usually made: "He (the bull) has stolen the women (the cows) so he is hiding out with them."

From late summer to early fall, all the buffaloes were together in small and large herds. Bull fights then were rare. With feed ripe and at its best at that time of the year, the buffaloes began to get fat. Long files of them leisurely went to water and back to feeding grounds. They traveled in single file and the buffalo trails, belly deep in places that can be seen to this day, were thus made.

At that time, too, the animals were at ease. During the heat of day they lay around a great deal because the big hunting days, which always molested them, had not arrived. They were not disturbed by hunters except occasionally for a supply of fresh meat.

When a herd of buffalo crossed a large river such as the Missouri, they swam across in small groups, one group after another. Because of the size of herds the leaders were, many times, already across and far on their way to new feeding grounds while the rear ones were still moving up to the river. It often took several hours before the last group was across. It is told that when buffaloes were swimming they blew water through their nostrils. This made a peculiar noise that could be heard for a long distance down stream.

An old woman, Makes Cloud, told this story:

"One time, late in the evening, I went to the Missouri river after water. We were camped east of Tule creek, which as the crow flies is twenty-six miles, so you know the distance is very great. It was a fine day and the evening was so still that odd noises could be heard in different directions. As I stooped to draw the water, I heard a strange noise. It seemed as though it was on or just under the surface of the water. When I got home with the water I described the noise that I had heard to my father and he said that this was made by buffaloes when swimming. He told others in the camp and the next day a large number of mounted hunters went to the river. They found a large herd had crossed at the mouth of Little Porcupine creek. The hunters had little trouble in killing them and brought back much meat which otherwise would never have been had."

The bellowing of bulls was another sound heard for long distances. Black Dog tells about it this way:

"Once, a group of us when young men were out hunting. Someone said, 'Listen! I hear a young buffalo bull bellowing.' So we listened very closely and all of us heard the low rumbling tone of a bull. We went in that direction for some time before we sighted a small group of buffaloes. The distance to that place the way it is mentioned now was about ten miles."

THE MAIN HUNTING TIME FOR THE ASSINIBOINE was in Join Both Sides Moon (October), at which time in good years the buffaloes were very fat and the bulls were still in the herds. This hunting was devoted to obtaining all the meat needed for drying and storing away for winter. The chase for robes came later.

When the Frost Moon (November) appeared, the bulls left the herds and gathered in groups and remained away from the main herds until the breeding time. In this moon the hides from four-year-old cows were taken. The hair was not prime but the hides were at their best for new lodges.

Buffalo calves started to drop about the full of the Frog Moon (April) and up to the time when Idle Moon (May) appeared. As far as is known no twins were ever seen, but it is told by a man named Crazy Bull that he saw a two-headed unborn calf while butchering a cow which was killed in the Sore-eye Moon (March). In a chase, calves never ran close to their mothers. All of them fell to the rear, so even if there were twins they were not noticed as such.

The hair on calves was of a yellowish color and remained that shade until they were almost a year old. Calves were called Little Yellow Buffaloes. Robes for children were made from these skins, which were tanned with the hair intact.

After a big hunt, in the early fall, a large number of motherless and deserted calves remained on the hunting ground. The cows deserted their calves as soon as the hunters gave chase and, usually, were in the lead of a running herd. The bulls ran just behind the cows while the yearlings and calves were in the rear. Some hunters claimed that the cows ran much faster than any other buffaloes in a herd, and that for this reason they were always in the lead. Yet, some said, the bulls ran just behind the cows to protect them and at no time were they ever left behind. They always kept right at the heels of the cows.

If a chase was near an encampment and many calves remained afterwards, boys mounted on yearling ponies and using their small bows and arrows staged a miniature chase, much to the delight of the hunters who looked on. Very young calves left motherless or deserted after a chase were known to follow the hunters back to camp.

When the calves were one year old, their coats turned from the yellowish color to a dark shade. A calf was so fluffy that it usually looked big for its age. Instead of calling calves yearlings the Assiniboines called them Little Black-haired Ones, or Fluffed-hair Ones.

Two-year-old buffaloes were called Two-teeth, having two full teeth at that age. Just before they reached the second year, their horns stood out and commenced to curve. At that age the tips of the horns were blunt, so they were also called Blunt-horns.

After they passed the second year their horns curved and a three-year-old was known as Curved-horns, due to the short, small, curved horns.

Small-built Buffalo was the name applied to the four-year-olds, which were also called Four-teeth. Robes, taken in the Middle (January) and Long Day (February) moons from those animals were considered the best of all. The hides were not too thick but the hair was fluffed out, silky and thick.

When the robe hunters rode into a herd, they looked only for "Small-built ones," both males and females, the ones with trim and neat bodies whose coats of hair looked much like fine fur.

At the age of six, cows were known as Big Females, which meant matured. The bulls were called, Horns Not Cracked, due to their fine polished horns. They spent much time polishing their horns by rubbing them against low cutbanks. Sometimes these bulls pawed down the upper sides of washouts and used that as polishers.

When hides were taken from the bulls they were skinned only to the shoulders and cut off, leaving out the parts that covered the humps. In skinning a mature bull the animal was laid in a prone position; then an incision was made along the back, starting a little above and between the tips of the shoulder blades and ending at the tail. When the skinning was completed, it was in two pieces.

Fat from matured animals, when rendered, was soft and of a yellowish color. The tallow from young buffaloes was always hard and white.

When buffaloes got very old they became thin. The horns, especially on the bulls, were cracked and there were deep grooves around the butts due to the brittle condition of the horns. Old bulls congregated in groups. They remained away from the main herds and usually died of old age or other natural causes because no one wanted their meat or robes.

Many odd things which happened and strange kinds of buffaloes noticed during the hunt were told about at gatherings afterward.

As SAID BEFORE, THE COLOR OF THE HAIR on all calves was yellowish and at one year it turned almost black. But a few retained their original color all through their lifetime. They were called, Yellow Ones, and most of them were females. They were not stunted but natural size buffaloes with an odd color. Robes made from the Yellow Ones were rare and an owner took much pride in presenting one to a prominent person.

White or albino buffalo were very rare. The number taken by the different bands became a record which was handed down through generations by word of mouth. Three were known to the tribe. The hide of one was brought back by a war party. It was not known whether the party killed the animal or took it from an enemy tribe in a raid. Another was owned by a northern band which, when the occasion arose, used a piece of it to make into a sacred headgear for a new headman. The third, a heifer, was only seen by several hunters who were returning to camp after a chase. Their horses were tired and no attempt was made to chase it. However, one of their number, whose name was Growing Thunder, followed the herd for some time but finally returned to the group and told how the herd seemed to guard the white one. He tried to get within shooting range of the animal but was unsuccessful. It remained at all times in the middle of the large herd. That was when the muzzle-loading type of firearms were being used for the first time by the Assiniboine.

Another kind known as Spotted Ones had white spots on the under side and on the flanks. Some had small white spots on one or both hind legs, usually near the hoofs. Only females were marked in this way.

The Small-heads were also females. They were of ordinary size but had very small heads and very short horns.

Curved-horns were both male and female. The bulls of this kind had short and very curved horns while the horns on cows were thin, long and curved. The tips, which curved out of sight into the hair made curved-horn cows look as if they wore ear rings.

Another old buffalo group was called Narrow-cows, on account of their narrow built bodies. From a side view they were no different from the general run of females, but in a chase, if one was in the herd, it was easily detected. In spite of their shape they were usually very fat and the meat good.

Mourning-cow was the name given to females whose forelocks, and sometimes the hair around the horns, was short and looked shorn. Among Assiniboine women it was the custom to cut their hair short as an act of mourning. Because some buffalo cows resembled women following that custom, they were known by that name. These cows got very fat but when alone they were much more vicious than other kinds. Mourning-cows would charge mounted hunters if they came too close. Meat from the animals was good but it was never eaten because of a belief that if any one ate the meat from a Mourning-cow knowingly, there would be death in the family. And if a hunter killed one of them, when he knew the cow to be of that kind, there would also be death and mourning in his family.

Hunters who saw such cows claimed that often in a chase where there was much excitement, dust, and hurried selections for a kill, Mourning-cows in the herd could not be detected. In the chase hunters had to kill from the rear. At an angle these cows looked no different from others. Because they were always fat they attracted hunters who generally selected "fat ones." After a chase was over, when the dust cleared and the hunters spotted their kills, the Mourning-cows were discovered if any had been killed.

BESIDES THE DIFFERENT KINDS OF BUFFALOES, there were strange ones seen or killed. These created stories that were told at gatherings and passed down for so many years that the first teller cannot be remembered.

Once a bull was killed whose thickness of fat around the neck was the width of a man's hand. It had a crease down its back which was never seen even on very fat buffaloes.

Among those killed in a chase was a four-year-old bull with a coil of spun hair rope that hung to one of his horns. Many gave opinions as to how the rope got there. Some said, "the rope must have been lost and the object attracted the attention of the bull. Out of curiosity he examined it more closely with one of his horns and it caught there." Others said, "Bulls were in the habit of polishing their horns on the edges of low cut banks, so maybe the rope, left on a bank, had been picked up that way." Still others stated, "A hunter was thrown against the bull during a chase and was hooked near the hip where the ropes in small coils were always carried and tucked under the belts. Perhaps, the coil hung to the horn when the bull hooked the hunter."

Another time a war party in camp near a river saw a herd of buffaloes coming to water. Some one said, "Look at the leader, there is something strange about the animal."

When the herd came closer, the men were still at a loss to know what really made the animal appear so different from the others. Two men crept near the watering place and when the herd came near, killed the strange-looking leader. The buffalo was an ordinary size bull, but the hair on its front legs was so long that parts of it dragged on the ground. The hair under the chin measured the length of a man's arm. Its forelock, too, hung far down and covered the eyes and almost to the tip of the nose. What made the buffalo look so strange was the way the long hair was blown, by the wind, to one side of the animal. From a distance it looked as though long shadows which tapered to points extended from its body.

Another story tells that one of the fetlock toes on a bull which was killed measured hand over hand seven times. It grew into a coil but, being on one of the hind legs, did not appear to have troubled the animal.

IN THE BUFFALO COUNTRY IS A ROCK which resembles a buffalo lying down. It was held sacred by the tribe and whenever a band passed by they always camped at some suitable camping place near the rock. Then the people placed offerings around it; some were in thanksgiving for things received or for good health enjoyed by their families, others asked for successful hunts, captured horses and other war achievements. The medicine men, who had the Spirit Buffalo for their helper, made their sacrifices for the welfare and prosperity of the people.

"The story of the Buffalo Rock," said Duck, "was handed down through the generations of our people. This is how it is told:

"A war party saw a small herd of buffaloes lying down on a knoll. The men quickly got out of sight, being all on foot. Two of the group were selected to kill a buffalo to replenish their meat supply.

"As the men crept near the herd, the animals remained motionless. They were grouped around an unusually large bull which the men knew was the leader of the herd. The men wanted to kill a young heifer and they made their way slowly and quietly toward the herd.

"As they drew closer, the buffaloes appeared to be the same size as when they first saw them. They again crept closer, then finally so near that the herd was easily within range of their arrows. But there was something mysterious about the group. The hunters looked at one another as they lay flat on the ground, each one waiting for the other to break the silence and make a suggestion. A spell seemed to hang over them. The small herd laid as motionless as before. Not one of them so much as moved its head.

"Without a word one of the men arose and the other quickly got to his feet. Both remained standing, not knowing just what else to do, for the herd remained stock still. None took flight. The men waved to the rest of the party and, by signs, told them to hurry over. When they came the two pointed to the herd still lying down.

"A council was held quickly and the party walked toward the herd. When they reached the spot, there was only a group of boulders where the buffaloes were first seen. But the large one in the center attracted the attention of the party. They saw that it did resemble a bull lying down.

"The war leader said, 'It is on war journeys, away from the smell of habitation, noise, bad talks and unclean persons when strange things are seen. This place is sacred. Let us sit down. I will fill and offer the medicine pipe to the buffalo and his group that they may look kindly upon us and when we

"IN THE BUFFALO COUNTRY IS A ROCK WHICH RESEMBLES A BUFFALO LYING DOWN."

get back to our people, this story will be told to them.' That is the story and, in my time, I have seen many sacrifices made to the Buffalo Rock."

Duck tells another story about the Rock, which happened before his time:

"Once there were no buffaloes in the Assiniboine country. There was want in every band. All other game was small and it took much to feed a band. So finally many families had to leave their bands and brave the attack of enemy war parties in order to seek food alone.

"One of these groups passed by the sacred Buffalo Rock and laid offerings there, asking for food. In the group was a young married couple, newly married. They were in the rear of the movers, the last to arrive at the Rock, because the man was ill and weak. His feet were sore from hunting afoot and also for the lack of food, so he walked with the aid of his wife.

"While the rest of the people moved on, the couple stopped some distance from the Rock. The man said, 'I will make an offering to the Rock but you must not come with me as no women are allowed near it.'

"So he crawled to the Rock and laid his offering with the others. He sat there in prayer, after which they continued the journey. Because they traveled slowly, they were left far behind. And so they were alone when they made camp near a small creek which was wooded with large willow patches.

"The woman cut and brought willows while the man crawled about helping her. Between them, they made a shelter of willows and leafy branches. A fire was built and the woman brought some water but there was no food to eat, so they just sat there in silence. The man sat with his eyes fixed on the fire, which was built just outside of the willow hut and close to the entrance. Without changing his gaze, he began to speak, but the words came with much effort: "'Seven moons ago, we were very happy. It was the first time that you and I were permitted to sit side by side. The buffaloes were plentiful then and my kills satisfied your father. It was planned that when one winter had passed you would set up our own lodge, made from the hides I had taken. But that is not to be. Much want has visited our people and they have scattered in many directions. Many families are even divided, but things are not made better by it.

"We are still together, but alone. Our people have gone on. We still wish much to always sit beside each other, although seven moons have passed since you became my sit-beside-me woman.

"'This willow lodge is going to be the one we planned that you would pitch. It was to be erected with much ceremony, according to the custom of our people. But now that part will be left out. In this lodge I will remain as I can go no further. You are still strong and must follow our people to save yourself. This is my wish.'

"She had sat at his right but farther to the side, near the entrance. She, too, had stared into the fire while he was speaking. Now she turned and came at once to his side. 'Together we will remain here,' she said, 'why should I go on? To whom? Seven moons ago you left the lodge of your mother and father and came to me to stay forever, and now, must I leave you? You————————'

"But whatever she was going to say was never finished. A peal of thunder, so loud, so hard that it seemed to rend something apart, came as out of nowhere. It shook the small framework which sheltered them and the ground where they sat.

"She threw herself against him and he covered her with a part of his robe. There they sat in silence, while the Thunder Birds made their presence known with lightning and thunder accompanied by wind and much rain.

"The storm did not last long. It was the kind of storm, the old men say, carried on by young and restless Thunder Birds who delight in coming suddenly upon a prey to destroy it; and also to cast fear into people who have not made their sacrifices to the Thunder Birds. Sometimes they came on a good mission and not always to destroy.

"After the fury of the storm, the rain settled down to a drizzle but the wind was still blowing so hard that it blew the fine rain into sheets. The fire was almost out. The woman went out to gather more dead willows to start it up again. In a short time she came running back, without fuel, and threw her arms around him. She clung to him breathless and speechless. The man was alarmed but gave her time to compose herself.

"After a time, with much excitement, she told of seeing three buffaloes standing close together in the shelter of the wooded creek.

"He said to her, 'It only grieves me and makes my heart heavy to know that there is meat so near and I sit here helpless.'

"Suddenly, but calmly, she said, "You are still strong in your arms and can draw the bow, I will carry you on my back and you can make the kill; the kill will save our lives and keep us together as before.'

"He seemed strong and happy as he got on her back. He whispered some words in her ear which brought a smile on her face. It was now nearly dusk but the wind and fine rain was still the same. With her burden she slowly made her way toward where she had seen the buffaloes. Softly she moved toward the spot and soon he saw them. They were huddled together, faced down with the wind, unconscious of a strangely mounted hunter who was behind them.

"The strength of past hunting days returned to the man. His left hand easily pushed the center of the bow away from the sinew-cord in his right hand and in a flash the arrow was gone. The three buffalo jumped in different directions and ran. But one of them went in a circling fashion, with its head down, then fell. A kill was made.

"The woman carried her husband over to it and, together they butchered it. When they were done she carried him back to their rude lodge and went back after choice parts for their immediate use.

"Once more they sat before the fire, but now, with smiles on their faces as of times past. Before they ate, he raised the broiled meat before him and called aloud the names of some of his departed relatives. He said, 'Come, sit with us and eat this meat which is given to us by the Sacred Buffalo, whose image lies close by. He has even asked the help of the Thunder Birds to drive the buffaloes close to our camp. We have much to give thanks for.'

"Early next morning the woman followed the trail of the people. When she arrived at their camp she told them of what had happened. Several hunters hurried back and killed the other two buffaloes which were found nearby. There was much rejoicing among the people and many pipes were filled and offered to the Buffalo Rock."

Some time ago this rock was moved to the nearby town of Malta. When U. S. Highway No. 2 was finished, it was taken back and placed near the highway just east of Lake Bowdoin, a short distance from its original site. An inclosure has been built around the rock by the Montana Highway Commission, and today the spot is an attraction to travelers.

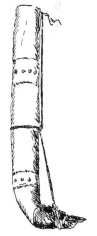

Even now, there are signs of offerings near the rock. They are made, strangely enough, not only by the Assiniboine but by Indians from other tribes going past who have heard the story of the Buffalo Rock.

BUFFALO HIDE SCRAPER

Fire Making

When fire first came to the Assiniboine is not known, but its use for warmth, for cooking and even for trapping game by encirclement on the prairie was of great value.

Several methods were used for starting a fire. One was as follows:

A block of ash wood was hollowed out to resemble a cup with the hole about one and a half inches wide and about two inches deep. Into this cavity was poured a mixture of rotten food and coarse, crushed rock, not more than an inch in depth. Two seasoned green ash sticks, squared to about one-half inch in diameter and about twelve inches long were placed together in the hole. The fire making was now ready to begin. Both sticks were held between the palms of the hands and, with fingers outstretched were revolved back and forth rapidly to cause friction. It was a skilled job for one person. But where there was a group, such as a war party, each member took turns until smoke started. Then the contents of the cup were poured out on dry bark, or if the camp was out on the prairie, on pulverized buffalo chips. By blowing on the smudge it soon blazed up into a fire.

A similar method was to use a much thicker block so as to have the hole deeper. This hole was loaded with the same mixture. Then using a single round stick, a fast up and down motion was made until smoke started in the rotten wood.

Because it was no easy thing to start fire by the friction method, once a fire was started it was kept alive as long as possible. Usually when the tribe moved to a new camping place the thrifty wives would have fire brands from their last camp fire carried by their grown boys and girls. As soon as a fire was started from these the shiftless women of a camp came to beg for a stick to start their fires.

"ON A WAR PARTY EACH MEMBER TOOK TURNS MAKING FIRE, UNTIL THE SMOKE STARTED."

Foods

There is an old Assiniboine saying, "The buffalo gives food from his flesh and clothing from his hide. The marrow, sinew, bones and the horns can be used by the people, so that a skilled woman can make many different kinds of food and the family does not eat the same thing each day. It is so also with the man who can make many things from the buffalo for use in war, hunting and pleasure. All these things the buffalo offers to the ones who heed the talks of the old men and the old women who know that the lives of the people and the growth of children depend on the buffalo."

People were satisfied with meat as their main food. This was prepared in many ways. Often it was roasted over an open fire. A piece consisting of several ribs was stuck on a stick with the other end of the stick in the ground near the fire. The meat was turned over and over until cooked. Some preferred to have pieces of fat laid on the tip, so that it melted and ran down into the buffalo flesh to give it flavor.

"Women made much dried buffalo meat ... hung on poles and turned over each day until it was as dry as a bone ... then packed away for future use."

Another method was to spread a piece of meat sliced thin on live embers until cooked.

Women also made much dried meat. To do this a large piece of fresh meat was first cut almost through the center and sliced each way until it was much larger and very thin. This was then hung on poles and turned over each day until it was as dry as a bone. The cured meat was then packed away for future use. It was also mixed with rendered marrow, then packed in sacks made from dried bladders and stored away. The dried meat was usually boiled until tender but it could be eaten uncooked without preparation. Often it was toasted, then pounded into a pulp and eaten dry with a piece of tallow or fat.

Meat dried from parts of the rump and from the two pieces on each side of the backbone of the buffalo was considered best. This was made into a pulp and mixed with rendered marrow and pounded chokecherries and served at feasts or ceremonial gatherings. It was called pemmican by the whites.

This story about the way men cooked meat was told by Last:

"Once, I was a member of a small war party that went on foot to the Piegan's country (near Glacier National Park). They were our enemies.

"Before we entered their country we rested one whole day, which was devoted to mending, looking over our equipment, and various other things that needed attention. My cousin, Red Feather, suggested that I prepare a boiled meal so I dug a hole in the ground about eighteen inches in diameter and twelve inches deep. I cut a piece of hide from the neck of a buffalo that we had just killed and lined the hole with it. I used pieces of buffalo ribs to peg the edges fast to the top of the hole and my pot was complete. I next filled it with water and placed pieces of different kinds of meat that each member wanted into the pot. I heated five rocks, larger than a fist, red hot, and by using a buffalo shoulder blade, I slipped one rock at a time into the pot, each time taking out the cooled rock, until the fourth one was in and the water began to boil. I left that one in and followed with the fifth. Then the water boiled hard enough to cook the meat. After a time I took the meat out and put buffalo blood into the broth and, with two more rocks, I cooked a soup that we all enjoyed.

"The women never cooked that way. It was a custom among men when they were away from home and wanted a change from the roasting method."

ANOTHER STORY IS TOLD BY BAD HAWK:

"My grandfather told how the men cooked buffalo ribs when they were out on trips. A hole about two feet square and a foot or more in depth was dug. Into that was laid a piece of ribs wrapped in green buffalo hide. This was then covered with dirt and a fire built over it.

"The cooking was timed this way: When the first fire had died down to embers, a fresh pile of fuel was laid on and when the last fuel was all burned, the meat was considered done. They called this method, 'Ribs covered and cooked with two fires.'"

Buffalo tongues were a great delicacy. They were generally eaten on special occasions, during feasts, or served in guest lodges to the headmen while in council. Families also served them to invited guests to honor some member of the family. While buffalo tongue was considered a choice dish, hoofs cooked tender were looked upon as poor fare and eaten only when there was not much of anything else to eat.

A HUMOROUS STORY IS TOLD ABOUT THIS.

A young man waited patiently to see his sweetheart one evening. Being uneasy, he tiptoed to the lodge and peeped in to see if the young lady was at home as men never entered the lodges of their sweethearts. He saw her eating boiled hoofs, the poor food. After she had finished, she came out. As she wiped the perspiration from her face, she said, to his dismay, "Sorry to keep you waiting, I have just finished feasting on buffalo tongue."

In the latter part of May a plant similar to rhubarb was gathered, cut up in small pieces and cooked with soup.

Wild turnips were rooted up with a pointed stick in the latter part of June and through July. Women both old and young, with the help of boys and girls, would spend a day at a time in gathering turnips. The boys and girls went ahead and located the turnip plants for their mothers, grandmothers or sisters who made up the party.

It was a common sight to see two or more children run on ahead to find turnip plants for their old grandmothers who, perhaps, could not see very well. The children vied with each other in finding the largest plants and took great pride in calling their grandmothers to view some especially large specimen.

Turnip plants were often combined with visiting. Young women, in pairs, strolled about in search of the turnips and at the same time exchanged news and gossip of the camp. Oftentimes a young lady carried a message from her brother to the lady of his choice and delivered it during such a time.

Turnips were peeled and eaten raw; or sliced and cooked into a soup, with pieces of fat added to give a rich flavor. The bulk of the turnips gathered were peeled, sliced and spread out on hides on the ground and dried. After they were thoroughly dried, they were packed away for winter use. Sometimes a portion of them was pounded and stored in that manner. The

"I have just finished feasting on buffalo tongue ..."

"Wild turnips were rooted up with a pointed stick."

cured turnips were boiled during the winter months very much as the white people cook dry beans. Being dry and hard they took a long time to cook. Children, while at play often chewed them.

Toward the end of the turnip season, juneberries were ready for picking and all who were able helped with the task. Although men never helped with any household duties, it was no disgrace for them to pick juneberries, as there was always danger of bears being in the berry patches. So the men acted as escorts and sometimes helped pick the berries.

Juneberries were spread out on hides, dried in the sun, and packed away. The grandmothers usually tanned fawn skins for use as berry bags, the skins from speckle-backed fawns being the most popular. When cured, these skins were tanned with the hair left on and all holes were sewed shut, except for one opening in the under side. The skin was filled and packed with cured berries and the opening sewed up. When completed the bag resembled a stuffed fawn. It was then presented to a favorite grandchild.

Fresh juneberries were often rubbed into pounded dried turnips. The mixture was cured in the sun and stored for winter food.

Chokecherry-picking followed the juneberries. Some of the berries were dried unpitted like the juneberries and some were crushed between two rocks. To do this a flat rock about eight inches in diameter, was placed in the middle of a hide spread on the ground. A woman, seated with the rock directly in front of her, took a handful of unpitted cherries with the left hand. A few were poured on the rock and crushed by a smaller rock made with a handle, which was held in the right hand.

This process was repeated until the desired amount was obtained. The crushed pile was then made into patties and dried in the sun.

Cured cherries, unpitted or crushed, were cooked as a soup and flavored with fats. Only crushed cherries were mixed with tallow and allowed to harden. They were also mixed with dried and pounded buffalo meat and rendered marrow fat.

After the berry season there was a lull until the buffalo hunting time in the early fall.

During that quiet period, the old women picked ripe rosebuds.

The Old Woman Who Tricked Her Captors

ONE FALL, SO LONG AGO NOBODY KNOWS HOW LONG, a band had killed a large number of buffaloes and the women were busy taking care of the meat. Jerked-meat was made, the fat rendered, the bones crushed and the marrow extracted by boiling. All this work fell to the women.

When, as customary, the camp crier came around and proclaimed that the camp would be moved to another location where there was new grass for the horses and clean campgrounds an old woman said, "Let me stay here just one more day to finish my rendering. I will follow the day after tomorrow." So the band left her at work and moved to the new campgrounds.

It was customary for women when working late into the night to use a torch made from a wad of buffalo hair soaked in grease, on the end of a stick. The stick, shoved under the woman's dress at the back extended beyond her head. As she leaned over her work the light was thrown forward.

On this occasion as the old woman sat with the torch illuminating her work, a group of eleven warriors came into her lodge. They said not a word but seated themselves as though they had been invited.

The old woman knew at once that the enemy was in her lodge, but she pretended to show no surprise. She pushed the embers to the middle of the fire and added more wood. Then she reached back and pulled a bag in front of her, from which she filled a large wooden dish with pemmican. She placed this in front of her nearest visitor, who took a large handful and then pushed the dish on to the next.

After all were served, the old woman looked up at the smoke hole. Then she glanced about the lodge, which indicated that the lodge smelled of smoke due to a change in the wind. She arose and with the torch in her hand went out as though to adjust the smoke flaps. But as soon as she was outside, she ran away from the lodge.

The enemy warriors soon noticed that she was not at the back of the lodge and rushed out. They saw the light of the torch moving away fast and knew that the old woman was in flight. Because the night was so black, the small torch looked larger than it was.

A short distance from the lodge was a cutbank with a drop of several hundred feet. It was towards this that the old woman ran. She had planned her escape. She waited a moment at the edge of the cutbank until her pursuers came close. Then she threw the torch ahead of her over the bank and stepped aside. Thinking she was running ahead over level country, the pursuers followed the torch and all of them fell to their death far below. The woman then walked on to the new campground of her band and told her story. At once men, with many women following, went to the scene. There eleven warriors lay dead. Scalps were taken and coups were counted. But the honor of the kill went to the old woman who made a story that is told even to this day—the old woman who tricked her captors.

Lodges, Clothing, and Ornaments

The first white men known by most of the Assiniboine people were the Hudson's Bay Company traders far up in the North country in what is now Canada. Long before other white men came they traded in cloth, blankets, beads, knives and other articles. But before the agents of the Hudson's Bay Company came the tribe depended entirely on wild game and nature to provide everything.

Lodges were then made from the tanned hides of matured buffalo cows. The number of finished hides required depended on the size of the lodge.

BUFFALO HIDE LODGE

An average lodge ranged from six to fourteen hides in size. Twenty hides made an extra large lodge, usually owned by a well-to-do bachelor. There were not many of that size, not because the material was scarce, but because they were cumbersome to carry and to handle.

Red Feather gave this description of his bachelor lodge:

"Before I was married, my mother, with the help of other women, made a bachelor's lodge for my use. It contained nineteen tanned hides and was very heavy. When the poles were set up and the covering was tied to the pole to be raised, it took three women to raise and set the covering in place. Of course, as you know, we men do not help with those things.

"It was thought that I lived alone in the lodge. I occupied the whole of the back part as my bed and the two sides were also supplied with bedding. But my cousins and friends who were also single were almost always with me, so usually several of us slept there every night. "My mother cooked for us and we ate in my large bachelor's lodge." Lodges were erected with pine poles. A tripod was set up and the rest of the poles were added. The number of poles used depended upon the size of the lodge. The bottom of a lodge was secured to the ground by wooden pegs made from the chokecherry tree. The front was laced together below and above the entrance, with pins made from the same kind of wood. The butt ends of the pegs and pins were carved and bands of bark in various widths were left intact as ornaments.

Assiniboine lodges always faced the south. Ventilation was regulated by two large flaps on each side of the smoke hole. Two extra poles governed the flaps from the outside. If there was smoke in the lodge due to a change in the wind one of the women went outside to regulate the draft.

A man never attended to anything in connection with the work in or about the lodge. If a man was seen helping a woman with any of her tasks, other men remarked to each other, "Since when has he become a woman. Hereafter leave him out at gatherings of the men for he may start teaching us to make women's dresses."

The regulation of the smoke draft was an old excuse for young unmarried women to go outside after dark to meet their sweethearts. If the girl knew that her lover was near her lodge, she would say, "It seems so smoky in here, perhaps the wind has changed. I must go out to adjust the flaps." And with that she attended to the chore and at the same time met the man. But, as she was not permitted to go very far away from the lodge, the two lovers stood close together and whispered to each other.

In winter the wall of a lodge for about four feet up from the floor was lined with tanned skins of the yearling buffalo. These skins were tanned like deer skins, the hair being removed first.

The lining of the lodges of well-to-do families, who had guests a great deal, were decorated with pictures of war exploits. Sometimes these picture stories told of the deeds performed by the host.

In these lodges several back rests were kept for special guests. They were made of peeled willows about three-fourths of an inch in diameter and two feet long. Laid horizontally the willow sticks were laced with hide or some other material around the outside and down the center. The top of this framework was then hung from a three-pole tripod so that the outside edges rested on the two front poles of the tripod. The third pole, in the back, regulated the slant of the back rest.

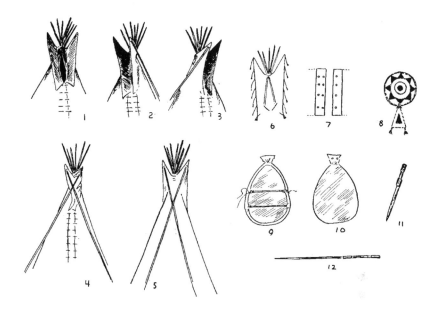

DETAILS OF LODGE CONSTRUCTION

Assiniboine lodges always faced the south. Ventilation was regulated by two large flaps on each side of the smoke hole, as indicated here in drawing (1) Fair Weather, (2) East wind and (3) West wind positions. Two extra poles governed the flaps from the outside. Drawing (4) indicates "nobody home" and (5) is a back view of the fair weather position of the poles and flaps. If there was smoke in the lodge due to a change in the wind, one of the women went outside to regulate the draft. Other details include: (6) Smoke flaps with tassel decorations. (7) Front lacing holes. (8) Side ornament. (9) Lodge entrance cover, inside view showing framework. (10) Outside view of lodge entrance cover. (11) Decorated lodge pegs, achieved by leaving bands of bark on the saplings cut for this purpose. (12) A lacing stick, used to close the front of a lodge by passing through the front lacing holes.

Those who took an active part in the social life of the tribe decorated their lodges with objects made by the women. These were sewed to different parts of the lodge on the outside. The edges of the smoke flaps were usually fringed with tassels covered with porcupine quills. More quillwork in large pieces was sewed to the back and sides. Sometimes holes were bored through the tops of the smoke flap holes. Buckskin strings were then laced through and tied so that the two ends hung as a fringe.

Lodges of warriors were painted with pictures that showed the war record of the owner. Medicine men painted their lodges with symbols of their religion.

Sometimes parents had a small lodge made for one of their children and gave a fee to a warrior who decorated it with pictures of one of his deeds.

ALL SKINS USED FOR ROBES WERE TANNED with the hair left on. The light robes for children and those used for extra bed covers were tanned skins of short yearlings or calves of the buffalo. On this, usually, hair was removed and the skins tanned. But many people preferred the skins of calves tanned with the hair left on. Two-year-old buffalo hides made the best robes when tanned by expert tanners. However, all women were not good tanners just as all men were not good hunters.

The skins from antelope, deer, elk and moose with the hair removed and tanned, were used for early day clothing. Antelope skins were the lightest in weight and moose hides were heaviest. The tanned skins of these animals were always known as buckskin.

The early people dressed very simply as far as style went. Men wore headgear of skins, sometimes decorated with feathers or strips of skin from small animals. They wore three-quarter length coats which also served as shirts. Their leggings were held up by a single strap, one end fastened on the outside of each one and the other wrapped around the belt or tucked under it. Robes were worn with the hair against the body so that the decorations on the under side would be seen as well as for warmth. Decorations, before beads came in with the Hudson's Bay traders and for a long time after, were done in colored quill work and paints. The clout, a pair of moccasins and the robe nearly always completed the dress of the man, except for the most severe weather.

The man's full dress for ceremonial use was the same in style but more decorated, with quills, feathers, hair and fur used. Some medicine men made their own headgear in the likeness of something they had seen in a dream or vision.

A woman's dress was in one piece, cut full and worn with a belt. Leggings were worn, held up by garters tied just below the knees. A woman's moccasins were made with high tops. Robes were used that ordinarily covered the head. A kind of hood and long furred mittens were worn in cold weather.

The buckskin dresses worn by women at dances were 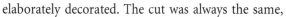 elaborately decorated. The cut was always the same, but the designs were different. Porcupine quillwork in many colors was the principal ornament. The bottoms were either fringed or trimmed with deer hoofs, only the shells of the hoofs being used. Sleeves were fringed to the elbow and the length of the fringe was a mark of value. Extra long fringe increased the value of the dress. Dresses trimmed with elk teeth were rare and valuable. Women told with much pride of the number of such dresses that had come into their possession during their lifetime.

Children wore dresses very much like their parents. During social gatherings, they, too, wore their decorated suits and dresses made from deer skins.

During the winter and spring, all people wore moccasins made from the tops of old lodges. The material was smoked during the life of the lodge. When footwear was made from it, it was not waterproof, but it never became hard or cracked from continuous use in a wet season like other leather. The soles and uppers of the winter-spring moccasins were of the same material. They were cut extra large in order to fit over heavy coverings of the feet. During the cold season, hair removed from buffalo hides was matted into pads of different thicknesses. The feet were wrapped with these pads and the large moccasins were worn over them. The regular ones worn in warm weather were close-fitted and soled with stiff, dry hides.

Cold weather moccasins were also made with high tops to protect the ankles. They were not decorated in any way being made only for service. Many applications of grease were put on moccasin soles to make them waterproof. That was a man's job.

Summer footwear for men and boys was low-cut. Sometimes this was partly decorated. Other times decorations covered the whole top and ran back to the heels. Women's and girls' moccasins although always having high tops were decorated like those of the man.

WOMEN PARTED THEIR HAIR IN THE MIDDLE and wore it in two braids. These either hung down in front or were tied together in the back by the ends. Sometimes the ends were tied at the back of the neck so that the braids formed loops and hung over each shoulder in front.

The old women painted their entire faces. A thin grease was first smeared over the face and then vermillion paint was put on. Young women merely painted their cheeks. The paint served two purposes—to improve their looks and to guard against sunburn.

Women among the northern bands tattooed their chins in strips which ran from the corners of the mouth downward with two or three vertical stripes in between and below the lips. A few of the women tatooed dots on their foreheads. These were from one-eighth to one-quarter of an inch in diameter and were done by men skilled at tatoooing. The large quills from the tails of the porcupines were used to prick the skin, then charcoal was rubbed into the spot. When healed over, the spots were a dark, bluish color.

Men wore their hair long in back and unbraided. The forelock was cut short and either hung to the brow or curled up. White clay was sometimes smeared on the hair to keep it in place.

When they were going to be out for considerable exposure in the weather, men painted their faces and hands to the wrists with vermillion paint. When at home they did not always paint themselves.

FOR JEWELRY, ARM BANDS MADE OF DEER ANKLE SKINS, with the hair and two "buttons" left on, were worn by young men. Old men wore earrings of twisted sinew, sometimes decorated with shells or ornaments which they made themselves. These were patterned after designs seen in dreams or visions. As a rule they were never copied. They also wore necklaces fitted snugly around the throat.

Among ornaments worn by women were garters with long quill-covered strings and shell tassels that hang to the ground.

The variety of ornaments as a whole was not large nor rich in colors until after the white traders brought beads, imported shells, metals, and many other things to the people.

Stone and Bone Articles

IN THE EARLY DAYS OLD MEN MADE ARTICLES of stone for a pastime as well as to make things that were needed.

From hard rocks they made such things as chokecherry and dried meat mashers, hones, and clubs to be used in warfare. Clubs and hammers were made from round stones grooved around the middle to hold handles that were sometimes incased in rawhide. The flat rocks used as anvils were natural ones selected for that purpose.

A soft grayish rock, similar to the red pipestone found in Minnesota, was made into pipes. These were used for ceremonials or on war parties, for general use in the guest lodges, and by the people.

After a pipe was fashioned and finished, it was covered with tallow and passed back and forth, slowly through the flames. As the fat melted away more was put on until the blackened grease penetrated the stonework. When it was entirely colored, the pipe was laid away to cool and later polished to a high gloss.

Kitchen utensils were made from large clam shells. Turtle backs were smoothed out and used for cups. Plates were more or less flattened pieces of wood.

The horns of elk were made into whip stocks. The men always carried whips, which hung from their wrists by loops and were also used as clubs.

Women fashioned horns into hoe-shaped tools that were used to scrape the hair off hides and skins.

Shields for warfare were made from the thick hide that covered the hump of the buffalo. When finished, they were decorated with paints and feathers.

Ropes were made of buffalo hide, cut around and around until the desired lengths were obtained. They were stretched and dried, then made pliable. A three-strand rope was made with smaller strips. Hair ropes were spun from the long hair of buffaloes.

Bags stuffed with deer hair and made into saddles were used by the old men. The stirrups were made of bent willows incased in rawhide.

Women made many sizes of folding food bags from untanned hides with the hair removed. They were decorated with colored paints in different designs and patterns. Large dried meat sacks with drawstring tops were made from coarse hides that were partly tanned.

Only the women tanned hides and skins. Sometimes very large buffalo hides were first cut in two and the pieces tanned separately, after which they were sewed together with sinew thread.

The intestines of bears were blown full of air and dried. Later, when rumpled they became white and soft resembling cloth. This material was used for ribbons, edging and various things which required such material.

ASSINIBOINE PIPES

Games

OLDER MEN PLAYED GAMES more for the wager than for amusement.

Several men would gather at a lodge to play one of their favorite games. The wagers consisted of clothing, ornaments, weapons, and even horses. Men sometimes lost everything they had taken along for wagers and left with only their clouts. Some of these games lasted for several days and nights.

An old one called the moccasin game was played by two teams. Four moccasins were placed in a row side by side in front of a player who put a small object inside of one of the moccasins. From the opposite team a representative came forward, a short stick in his hand, and tried to guess which moccasin contained the hidden object.

Young men amused themselves at target shooting with blunt arrows. In one game a hoop, laced so that a square hole was formed in the center, was used. This was rolled, the hole forming the target.

In another game, a young man shot an arrow into a bank leaving it there as a target. The others in the group then tried their skill in hitting it or putting another near it.

The slide stick game still played by boys was very interesting. A group of boys went to the woods and each selected about ten willow sticks cut in three- and four-foot lengths. The bark was stripped off in long lengths and put back on the sticks by wrapping, to form different patterns. When all had wrapped their sticks, a fire was kindled and the sticks were passed back and forth through the flames. When the flames had blackened the sticks completely, the wrappings were removed and the patterns were then visible. After a day or two, when the sticks were dry, the game was played by throwing them from different positions.

To start the slide stick game, the small end of a stick was held between the thumb and second finger with the tip of the index finger on the end of the stick. There was a space of three inches between the index finger and the second finger and thumb. Each boy threw one stick in a certain direction, aiming at no particular target, but merely to get distance. When each one had thrown a stick, the group walked forward and each player picked up his stick. The owner of the stick that went the farthest won the right to select a position at which he was most skilled and, also, the right to the first play. If the player won he still had another chance and led as long as he won at each throw.

Some of the positions from which the sticks were thrown are as follows:

The player extends his left foot in front, toes up and heel firmly placed on the ground. He first touches the butt end of the stick on the ground, then slides it across the left instep with such force that the stick springs upward and glides into space. The same play was repeated using the right instep and then across the tops of both feet, placed with the toes crossed.

The game required a great deal of balance to carry out the different positions played. Each boy kept count of the number of times that his sticks fell ahead of the others. As they all had from six to ten sticks each, they chose a stick from their bundle suitable for a certain position, For example, a long stick would be the kind to use for throwing across the instep; a short one for throwing down on smooth hard ground and bouncing off into the air.

Boys also played with mud sticks made from willows. They were from eight to ten feet long and about one inch in diameter at the butt end. The player carried a ball of mud in the crook of his left arm. A small piece of it was rolled with the palms into a ball and stuck on the tip of the stick which was held in the right hand and swung backward. The arm was brought forward with a quick motion to make the throw. The piece of mud was thrown at objects or over the water for distance throwing. Sometimes two groups of boys made war on each other with the mud sticks for weapons. Young men sometimes even used mud sticks to kill small feathered game.

Tops were made from the tips of buffalo horns and were spun on the ice. They were kept in motion by striking them with quick blows from lashes tied to short sticks. The lashes were applied to make the tops spin faster and faster until they hummed. Then they were thrown with the stick handles against a steep bank. The winner was the one who threw his top the highest.

Women played a game with a large ball knocked about with a crooked stick. The ball was first placed between two groups of women with from six to ten players in each. One from each side stood near the ball and at a given signal both struck at it with their clubs. Each player tried to knock it toward

POSITIONS OF BOYS SLIDE STICK GAME
PICTURED HERE ARE SIX POSITIONS USED IN PLAYING THE SLIDE STICK GAME, SO COMMON
IN OLDEN DAYS AMONG THE ASSINIBOINE. TOP, LEFT, PLAYER IS STARTING THE GAME.
WITH THE SMALL END OF A STICK HELD BETWEEN THE THUMB AND SECOND FINGERS
EACH PLAYER THROWS A STICK ENDEAVORING TO GET AS MUCH DISTANCE AS POSSIBLE.
THIS DETERMINES THE FIRST PLAY, WITH THE WINNER SELECTING HIS FAVORITE POSITION
FROM AMONG THE OTHER FIVE PICTURED HERE, DESCRIBED IN DETAIL IN THE TEXT.

her side. The side that got the ball took it on toward its goal line which was about fifty steps from center, with their opponents in hot pursuit. When those carrying the ball were over taken, there was a lively skirmish with much noise from the striking of club against club.

Before the game started, players collected such articles as trinkets or clothing, usually among themselves, and made up a wager which was divided into two piles. The players on one side had their collection in one pile, and the players on the opposite team had theirs in another.

At the end of each game the wagers were settled and new ones put up for the next game. Sometimes the spectators put up the wagers.

An indoor game played by women was the odd-stick game. Forty-one small peeled sticks about twenty-four inches long were used. There were two players. One, with hands behind her back, divided the bundle into two bunches, one in each hand. Then, crossing the two bunches of sticks in front of her, she extended them to the other player who took her choice. Each player counted the sticks in her bunch and the one who got the even number of sticks won. It was not necessary for the winner to have the greatest number of sticks.

Women usually made an entertainment of this game which lasted all evening with a lunch always served. Men were not allowed to even look in. When the game became very entertaining, peals of laughter could be heard, much to the discomfiture of the young men who often waited patiently for their sweethearts far into the night.

Boys' Mud Stick Game

PART IV

HUNTING

Bows and Arrows

The Tribal Hunt

Traps and Snares

The Chase

Story of Fast Runner

Hunting Deer

Bows and Arrows

BEFORE THE WHITE MAN'S GUNS WERE TRADED FOR, the bow and arrow was the principal weapon of the Assiniboine both for hunting game and in warfare. On long trips, extra bows were always carried by the warriors.

Bows were made from chokecherry, ash, and burr-oak or scrub oak. The last named was considered the best material for a dependable bow.

A first-class bow was made with much care by the men. The length was varied to suit the user. After the bow was shaped, the back was grooved diagonally, at intervals, the full length. That was done to hold the glue, which was made by boiling tendons of the hoofs and other cords from the buffalo into a jelly.

A thin coat of this glue was spread over the entire back of the bow and two whole wet sinews were then pasted on, with the butt ends together at the middle and the thin ends extending each way. More glue was spread over the whole back and immediately sprinkled with powdered white clay. After that coat was partly dried, more glue was put on and the bow again sprinkled with clay. This treatment was repeated several times. The number of coats determined how strong the bow would be. Some men used very flexible bows while others did not want bows of the type which, after a shot, sprang back and snapped the wrist with the bow string. Others, who had strong wrists, preferred heavy bows because in a sudden draw a strong man could break a bow which was too light.

After several coats of the glue mixture had been put on, the bow was a grayish transparent color. To finish the job, the back was decorated in different designs with colored paints. Then it was coated once more with glue to preserve the colors. The middle of the bow was wrapped with a piece of buckskin the width of the hand. At the top was tied some colored horse mane, or human hair taken from an enemy.

On some bows a sharpened prong, made from the horn of an elk, was attached to one end. These were used in battle as bayonets after a warrior had shot away all his arrows.

Six kinds of arrows were used, the difference being in the points. They were the flint, the bone, the iron, the arrow that tapered to a sharp point, the dull-pointed target arrow, and the knob-headed arrow used either for target or game.

The second-growth woods most used for arrows were the juneberry and chokecherry. Currant was not often used because, while it was smooth and straight without any knots, it was easily split.

Arrows from juneberry were the finest. This second-growth wood was straight, without a knot. It was also branchless and of uniform diameter for about three feet. Fully cured, the wood resembled hardwood.

The customary method of measuring the length of an arrow was to grasp the stick so that the butt was even with the bottom of the left hand, then measure hand over hand, six times. This length usually measured twenty-four inches.

The feathers used for arrows were taken from the wings of large hawks and eagles. They were split in two, the edges scraped thin, then glued to the arrow. The ends were fastened in place by wrapping with wet sinew. Two halved feathers were generally used; three and four were also popular. The long, single half-feather pasted on spiral fashion was not often used.

A pointed arrow without feathers, when shot, nose dived. But the knob-head one was often used without being feathered, as it was practical either

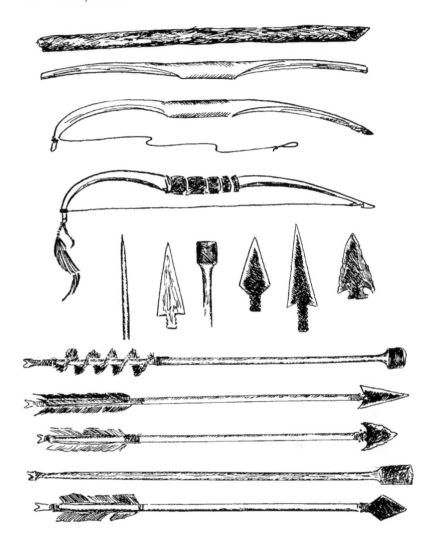

BOW, ARROWS, AND ARROW POINT TYPE

IN DAYS BEFORE THE WHITE MAN, THE ASSINIBOINE'S LIVELIHOOD WAS DEPENDENT LARGELY ON THE BOW AND ARROW. FINE CRAFTSMANSHIP WAS INCORPORATED IN THE ITEMS REPRESENTED ON THIS PAGE. AT TOP ARE SEEN FOUR STAGES IN THE MAKING OF A BOW. THE SIX ARROW POINTS INCLUDE: AN OLD-TYPE POINTED ARROW STICK, ENTIRELY OF WOOD; A HUDSON'S BAY METAL POINT; KNOB-HEADED TARGET AND SMALL GAME TYPE; TWO OTHER METAL POINTS; AND AN ANCIENT CHIPPED-STONE POINT. VARIOUS METHODS OF FEATHERING AND SHAPING THE ARROW SHAFTS PICTURED BELOW, INCLUDE: KNOB ARROW WITH SINGLE HALF-FEATHER FASTENED IN SPIRAL FASHION, STEEL-POINTED ARROW WITH THREE HALF-FEATHERS, OLD-TYPE FLINT ARROWHEAD AND TWO HALF-FEATHERS, THE PLAIN KNOB TYPE AND A DULL-POINTED METAL ARROW WITH TWO HALF-FEATHERS.

way. Boys used the knobbed arrow for practice and sports. Thirty arrows made a full quiver.

Small bows and arrows were used by boys at an early age. Their bows usually were made of chokecherry wood. Tall slough grass, dried and cut to suitable lengths. served as arrows. That kind was shot with the hard butts or joints against the bow string.

The story is told of a Sioux war party that attacked a small camp of Assiniboine who were away from their regular band on a hunt.

The men were out after buffaloes, when the Sioux, who saw that the men had all ridden away, charged the camp and began to massacre the women and children. A woman, with her four-year-old son on her back, fled toward the heavy timber nearby. Close behind her was a Sioux warrior, with a stone club, ready to strike. The little boy had his bow and grass arrows and his mother said to him, "My son, my son, shoot the enemy with your arrow."

The boy placed an arrow to his bow and let fly. The arrow pierced the eye of the Sioux and, while he spun around in agony, the woman ran into the timber and was saved. From that time on, the old men of the tribe, in giving advice to boys and young men, said, "Wherever you go, even for a short distance, always take your bow and arrows with you. In your spare moments, look over your bow and see that the bow-string is ready for use and your arrows are all straight and well kept. You never know when you may need them. You may be like the little boy who saved his mother as well as himself."

THE LITTLE BOY WHO SAVED HIS MOTHER FROM THE SIOUX.

The Tribal Hunt

THE NORTHERN BANDS OF ASSINIBOINE were noted for successful buffalo traps. By that method sufficient meat could be gotten at one time for ample distribution even among a large band. The whole tribe took part in the event.

When a chase of that kind was proposed a suitable lay of the land was looked over. If the band was already camped near a timbered creek, a ravine with steep sides and one that gradually leveled off into the prairie country was selected. If the encampment was on the prairie, an eroded creek was used as a trap.

The most common location was the timbered site. The mouth of a ravine was enclosed with a circular stockade. The trees and brush were cleared and only trees that were in line to form a circle were left to serve as uprights. A tree was also left in the center for the medicine pole.

"THE MOUTH OF A RAVINE WAS ENCLOSED WITH A CIRCULAR STOCKADE ... PEOPLE CONCEALED THEMSELVES BEHIND THE WILLOW ENCLOSURES ... WAITING FOR THE BUFFALO TO BE COAXED AND DRIVEN IN FOR THE KILL ..."

Loose brush was piled around the enclosure. From the entrance two lines led away along the steep sides and gradually widened out for about a mile. Willows tied together in large bundles and set upright at intervals formed the lines. In winter, piles of snow were used.

A good-sized lodge was pitched near the enclosure and the master of the ceremonial hunt with his helpers took their places in it. Four days and nights were spent in meditation, fasting and the singing of buffalo songs.

The men invited to the lodge by the master were medicine men who had power from the Sacred Buffalo, men who through visions had been promised help from the Buffalo for sacrifices that they had made to him in times past. The people always relied on their medicine men and their helpers who were able to call the buffaloes in.

In the back part of the lodge was placed a buffalo head, and dried sweet grass smoldered in front of it throughout the entire ceremony. Many offerings were brought to the lodge by the people. These were offered to the spirits of the buffaloes by the master, in exchange for their flesh.

After the fast, well-known hunters were invited to the lodge and told to locate the herd. Several rode away as scouts, and as soon as a herd or part of a herd numbering about 200 buffaloes was found, the hunters went out to drive it in.

In the meantime the people concealed themselves behind the long rows of willows and awaited the coming of the herd.

Riders who drove the buffaloes to the one who was to lead them stayed far behind after the herd was on its way. Their part in the hunt was over.

When the herd was headed in the direction of the trap, a lone rider stationed a distance from the ends of the herd said something like, "Yip! yip! yip!" At the call, the buffaloes stopped, raised their heads and looked in his direction. Then the rider turned toward the trap and the herd followed him.

He watched the movement of the herd and gauged his pace accordingly. Usually it followed slowly, but sometimes the herd would trot so that the rider had to urge his mount along to keep the same distance ahead. If a rider rode ahead at a pace faster than that of the buffaloes, they finally ceased following. Or, if the rider was too slow, the buffaloes caught up and would shy away from him in another direction. The rider had to keep the right distance between himself and the buffaloes.

At some traps the medicine man, who was in charge of the ceremonial hunt, went out on foot to meet the buffaloes and, instead of calling to them, he sang a buffalo song. When they started in his direction he walked toward the trap between the wings and into the enclosure, sometimes with the whole herd following him. He then went out of the pen through a small opening made for that purpose. Being a medicine man, he had the right to invite the buffaloes to the trap in that manner.

When the last of the herd had passed the ends of the wings, one of the persons concealed behind the willows exposed himself just enough to be noticed by the buffaloes in the rear so that they then moved into the main herd and, in turn, hurried the others along. As they moved towards the trap, the concealed persons, one after another, followed the example of the first one as the rear of the herd passed their stations. A slight movement was enough to be noticed by the buffaloes. To be seen too much would result in a stampeded herd.

The leader turned aside at the entrance allowing the buffaloes in the lead to jump into the enclosure. These were followed by the herd.

CEREMONIES FOR A SUCCESSFUL BUFFALO HUNT

When the last of them had gone in, several persons concealed nearby, rose up and rushed to the entrance. These men stood within the gap and waved untanned hides at the buffaloes to keep the herd in while other men closed up the entrance with logs, branches and brush.

As the buffaloes milled around in the trap, they were killed with arrows. When all had been slain, the head medicine man took a portion of the offerings of braided and dried sweet grass and touched each one of the dead buffaloes with it. In later years red flannel or some other cloth was used.

There were times when the herd broke through the wings during the approach or got out of the trap at some weak spot in the stockade. When that happened, a group of riders stationed nearby for the purpose had to kill the buffaloes in a chase.

The riders were the first to be called in and told to select their buffaloes. They always chose the fat ones and marked their ownership with staffs laid on the dead animals.

The people then butchered, and the meat was distributed among them according to their needs. Sometimes entire buffaloes were allotted to families. All tongues and hearts were piled inside the ceremonial lodge. These were later given out to the ones who came and asked for them. Choice parts of the buffalo were laid aside and given to the master and his helpers.

There was always a scramble of men for the arrows, each one keeping those he could get.

After the meat was taken care of, the inside of the enclosure was cleaned. Leftovers were piled on the hides and dragged out and away from the trap. The whole place was then sprinkled with new dirt or, if in winter, snow was thrown on.

That kind of hunt usually started in the fall and, if a trap was in a suitable place and the drives were successful, it was used many times over throughout the winter.

THE OLD MAN, LAST, TOLD THIS STORY ABOUT A HUNT WHEN BUFFALOES GOT AWAY:

"Our band, the Dog Band of the Prairie, had a trap near Woody Mountain, now in Canada. Once when the buffaloes were nearly all in the enclosure, a young man, the son of Flint Hand, was at his position on one side of the main entrance.

"Before the last of the herd had gone in he rushed forward too quickly

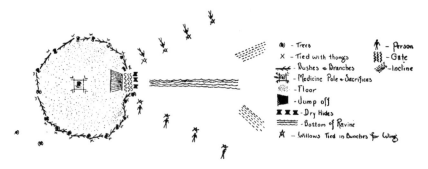

Legend:
- ⊛ – Trees
- X – Tied with thongs
- ⋘ – Bushes & Branches
- 🔯 – Medicine Pole & Sacrifices
- ⋮ – Floor
- ▮ – Jump off
- ⚹⚹⚹ – Dry Hides
- ≈≈≈ – Bottom of Ravine
- Ж – Willows Tied in Bunches for Wings
- 个 – Person
- 🔲 – Gate
- ⋙ – Incline

DIAGRAMMATIC DRAWING OF A TYPICAL BUFFALO TRAP

with his dry hide and frightened the herd. The rear ones broke back with the result that the whole herd got away.

"Then someone shot an arrow into the young man and several more persons followed suit. The man was killed. I don't believe he meant to scare the herd, but he did and the penalty had to be hard. Perhaps he had never taken part in a drive before and was too anxious.

"Flint Hand came forward and killed the man who had been the first to shoot his son. Then he, too, was immediately killed. From then on, relatives took sides and several women were killed.

"A niece of Flint Hand, with a baby on her back, ran toward the fighters, beseeching them to stop. By that time much blood had been shed and, as she advanced, one of the men shot her. The arrow, which entered her head through one eye, killed her.

"There was much confusion and the whole camp broke up and formed into many groups, scattering to new camping places to forget the affair."

A STORY IS TOLD OF ANOTHER WAY OF TRAPPING A HERD. In this the band known as the People of the North killed a large herd of buffaloes, although there were only seven horses in the entire camp, owned by a few prominent families.

On the advice of the Soldiers, an organization that kept order in a band, all the lodges were pitched close together in a circle. The lacings below the entrances were left unfastened and the corners spread apart each way and tied to the flaps of adjoining lodges to form on enclosure. An opening was left at one side from which extended two wings walled with lodge coverings and fastened to poles.

Riders on the seven horses rode out and drove a large herd of buffaloes towards the camp. One of their number acted as a leader for the herd.

The dogs were tied up out of sight and all the people remained in their lodges while they waited for the arrival of the herd. At last the rider came, at the head of the herd, and rode between the wings into the camp circle with the buffaloes following him. When the herd was all within the circle the riders stood guard at the entrance while it was being walled over with parts of the wings. Then the seven riders rode into the herd and as the buffaloes ran around within the camp circle they were killed with bows and arrows.

Never before had a trap of that kind been seen, for no medicine man had taken part in the affair. Because the Soldiers had charge of it there was no religious ceremony. Many were the songs of praise and thanks giving sung by the old people for the Soldiers who had managed the affair so successfully.

AN EXAMPLE OF THE CONFIDENCE which the people placed in the ceremonial hunt is indicated in another story.

When the Sioux were at peace with the Assiniboine, a band of Sioux were camped near where the Canadian boundary is today. Buffaloes were scarce and the wandering band was large. There was starvation in the camp. And so the Sioux, who did not hunt by the trap method, sent a runner to the nearest Assiniboine band with an offer to a medicine man named Tapo, which meant Moose-Nose.

The message said that if Tapo would conduct a trap for them and was successful they would present him with two of their women.

A half-circle-shaped cutbank was selected by Tapo to serve as the trap. But instead of the bundles of willows at intervals, which usually formed the wings, lodges were spread out and connected by poles. Thus, two continuous walls were made. This type of trap was called "The Lodge Trap."

As the herd came between the walls into the trap, the entrance was closed behind them by drawing the lodge walls together. The buffaloes were then shot from the rim of the cutbank by the Sioux hunters.

Tapo had conducted a successful buffalo trap and the Sioux kept their promise. They presented two women to him to be his wives.

IN WINTERTIME WHEN HUNTERS WENT OUT IN DEEP SNOW, they used snow shoes and dressed in white wolfskins which made them almost invisible. In that

"In wintertime when hunters went out in deep snow they dressed in white wolfskins. In that way they could approach very close to the herd ..."

way they could approach very close to the herd and kill many buffaloes.

When the snow was very deep, and the coulees were all blown full, and the ridges were almost bare, the buffaloes were driven along the ridges into the coulees. There the hunters on snowshoes killed many that had floundered in the drifts. The fresh meat kept the people well and happy during long winter months.

Traps and Snares

TRAPS AND SNARES WERE FREQUENTLY used for killing most kinds of small game.

Coyotes, foxes, skunks, badgers and the other prairie animals of this kind were taken in traps made in this manner:

Two rows of wooden stakes were driven in the ground about two feet apart. The rows were three feet long, two feet high and open at each end. The south opening served as the entrance. A pole was imbedded in the ground across the entrance to form the threshold. Another, three feet longer, was laid directly on top. The top pole, being longer, extended two feet on one side and a foot on the other. Two large stakes were then driven, one on each side, which held the poles in place and also served as door posts.

Split poles, slightly longer than the enclosure, were laid lengthwise between the two rows of stakes, with the butts resting on the top pole at the entrance. Several large boulders were then laid on top for weight. To open up the entrance, the short projecting end of the top pole was raised, the longer end resting on the ground. That made a horizontal V-shaped opening which was propped in place with a short round stick with the bottom placed on top of the threshold and the tip under the top pole. The trigger was a sharp-pointed stick about eighteen inches long, the butt of which was flattened out and placed directly under the prop stick so that the end of the trigger was sandwiched between the threshold and the lower end of the

prop stick. A piece of fresh meat was stuck on the sharp end of the trigger. The trap was then set. It resembled a slant-roofed shed.

When an animal passed through the entrance, the bait was pulled away. The prop stick slipped and the roof came down on the animal. The weight was usually enough to kill it.

To catch snowshoe and cottontail rabbits a single snare made with a loop of twisted horsetail hair was used.

One end of the loop was tied to the center of a round stick about two feet long. The stick was placed crosswise in the bushes or small trees beside a well-beaten trail in the woods. The loop was large enough to slip over the head of a rabbit. As the rabbit ran along the trail it was caught in the loop and strangled.

During the late fall mornings prairie chickens were in the habit of congregating in large numbers. These were called "chicken dances," because the male birds strutted around and made a lot of noise.

Snares for trapping the birds were made by driving two stakes into the ground about eight or ten inches apart and leaving them a foot above the ground. A crosspiece was fastened on top and to that a horsetail hair cord was tied and the loop formed. A number of these snares were built close together. As the chickens in their dance ducked in and out between the stakes some were caught in the loops and strangled.

Ducks were taken in the summer just before the young were ready to fly. As the young ducks dived and swam under water, they were detected by the movement of the wiregrass. A group of men wading abreast across the slough reached down where there was such movement, grabbed them and wrung their necks.

YOUNG DUCKS WERE TAKEN IN THE SUMMER.

The Chase

THE HUNT WAS THE MAIN SOURCE OF LIVELIHOOD for every tribe. Although other game was eaten, buffalo meat was most used.

When meat was plentiful in camp, the men hunted alone or in groups as they desired. But as soon as the supply was low and buffaloes were scarce no one was allowed to hunt alone or when he pleased.

Scouts were then sent out. When a herd of buffaloes was located by the scouts, hunters were called together to hunt in a group. In the course of the chase each killed one or two animals according to his needs. The owners of buffalo runners often loaned their horses to good hunters who killed buffaloes both for themselves and for the owners of the horses.

When hunters approached a herd, word was passed along, "Pick out the fat ones and kill one or two extra. Remember, there are old men and women at home who are looking this way for their meat."

While the chase was in progress grown boys on horseback took pack horses to the scene to bring the kill to camp.

Hunting buffaloes on horseback with bow and arrows was not easy, nor could everyone make a kill in this manner. The horse must be a fast animal, used to the hunt, forever on the alert, and watchful of the animal just ahead. Often if a buffalo was crowded, it would suddenly charge the horse. A good horse would jump out of the way in an instant.

An experienced rider knew that this might happen and he guarded against being thrown amongst the herd, possibly with fatal injuries.

Duck tells this story of a hunt:

"Before I was married I hunted a great deal, more for the sport of it than for food. This was after we had guns.

"An old man, named Medicine Cloud, owned a very good buffalo runner. He told my father that at the next hunt I could use his horse.

"A very large herd of buffaloes crossed the Missouri River at the mouth of Little Porcupine Creek and were moving north up that creek. The leaders were already so far ahead that they looked about the size of dogs. Across the river the rear ones could not be seen, so many were there in the herd. If the ones in sight had been counted the number would easily have reached one thousand. The buffaloes had separated into small groups of ten to fourteen, and when I got to them hunters were already amongst the herd and a chase was on here and there.

"A small group of cows and bulls ran out of a coulee and I took after them. Right away I knew the horse was a trained buffalo runner. His ears were continually moving about and he watched the group ahead.

"In a short time I caught up to them but I hadn't taken my gun out. I stuck the gun under my belt and was carrying it crossways with the stock at my right.

"Without warning a bull jumped right in front of my horse. The horse, being experienced, was out of the way in a flash, but I was pitched off and landed across the hump and behind the horns of the bull. He gave a snort and reared up in the air, which threw me, and I landed on my back several steps away. The fall knocked the wind out of me. While I spun about trying to get my breath a hunter rode up and said, 'I saw your misfortune and was afraid the bull would attack you. Here, I have caught your horse.' Sometimes horses were better buffalo hunters than their riders."

THERE WERE MANY OTHER DANGERS. The story is told that a man named Slanting was chasing a herd of buffaloes. He had not made his kill but was right behind ready to make a selection. The dust raised by the chase was so dense that only the animals in the rear could be seen. Without warning his horse bolted and ran for several hundred paces before he could bring him under control.

When the dust had cleared away the rider saw why his horse had shied. The whole herd in their blindness to escape had run over a cutbank and many were killed, while others crawled around with broken limbs and backs.

Slanting dismounted and led his horse to the bank. He surveyed the scene below, then rode back to camp and told of the incident. People hurried to the coulee and killed the ones that were injured. Then there was a great butchering of the buffaloes.

Several of the old men tracked the hunter's horse. Signs were easy as the ground was badly torn up where the horse had made the turn.

At that point it was almost impossible to see the edge of the bank which seemed to be a part of the prairie beyond. They found that the animal had turned in the nick of time.

For many years rocks could be seen that had been placed at each hoof print by the old men, and whenever a camping party was in that part of the country the story was always told. To this day the place is known as "Where Slanting ran the buffalo herd over the cutbank."

IN LATE SUMMER THE BUFFALOES AS A RULE got very fat and lazy and lay around in groups. At this time men who were the fastest runners hunted them on foot. They enjoyed the sport and it was a great honor among hunters to take buffaloes in that manner.

"WITHOUT WARNING A BULL JUMPED IN FRONT OF MY HORSE. ... I WAS PITCHED OFF AND LANDED ACROSS THE HUMP AND BEHIND THE HORNS OF THE BULL..."

These hunters were all young unmarried men who took good care of their physical condition and owed their ability as runners to some supreme Being. Old men who were great runners gave instructions and "made medicine" for the younger men. A small pouch containing the medicine was always carried under the belt at the right side. The young men made sacrifices and gifts to the old masters in return for these instructions and use of the herbs that would make them fast runners.

On a still, hot day the men planned this kind of chase. They stripped of all clothing except moccasins and clouts and tied their hair with bands on top of their heads. Some carried knives in their hands and others carried them in the sheath.

The hunters stalked a herd with much care so as to get as close as possible, then dashed at them and by the time the surprised herd had scrambled to their feet to flee, the runners were nearly amongst them. The fat buffaloes were soon winded and ran with their tongues out. The men ran close in and slashed their flanks until they dropped dead.

Slanting's escape.

After this they were butchered. Tall grass was cut and spread on the ground near each animal slain. The parts of meat were laid on it and the hide was used to cover it over.

Word was then sent to the camp and either horse or dog travois were brought to carry the meat to the lodges. Sometimes, when the meat was to be left overnight, each hunter marked his pile with some object to show ownership. Also, flags were made of brush or parts of their clothing and placed on top of the piles to scare away marauding animals and birds.

WHEN A MAN CAME BACK FROM A HUNT HIS WIFE MET HIM. If he was successful and came home laden with the kill, it was one of his happiest moments. He slid off his mount and his wife led him into their lodge, where he lay down. She unpacked the horses, picketed them where the grass was good, and gave only needed attention to the kill. She then devoted all her time to him; first taking off his moccasins, washing his feet, and powdering them with dry vermillion-colored earth paint. Then she removed all his clothing and, while he wrapped himself in a robe and rested, she prepared hot food for him. As she waited on him she carried on a pleasant conversation and talked of things agreeable to him. There was peace and contentment in the lodge.

If the man was a well-to-do person who had three wives, the wife who always accompanied him to social gatherings was the one who took him into the lodge and attended to his wants. The other two saw to the care of the kill and the horses. One remained and cared for the meat while the other led the horses out to grass. If the man owned a buffalo runner, the women saw to it that the horse was rubbed down with soft sage before it was allowed to graze.

But if the man came back empty handed his reception was cold. Whether he was poor or well-to-do, his wife or wives scornfully went at once to the

lodges of their parents or visited at other lodges. The man had to take care of his horses himself, dry his moccasins, and then get a cold meal.

In order to avoid an unpleasant welcome many men joined the Deer Society, a men's religious organization. They received a bracelet, with an ornament attached to it, which they wore during the hunt. The ornament was a charm made from the short prong of a deer horn. Only when a hunter was on his way back empty handed, did he resort to the actual use of the charm. When he saw game he wore it around his left wrist while making the kill.

The bracelets were made only by old society officers. A suitable offering, which was a fee for the maker, was made by the recipient. Women, children and male non-members were never allowed to touch the bracelet because,

"When a man came back from a hunt ... laden with the kill, it was one of his happiest moments."

as a part of the sacred regalia of the Deer Society, this was forbidden.

When a meeting was held all of the regalia used by the Society were passed back and forth over a burnt sweet grass offering, in full view of the audience, to purify them. All members were expected to pass their bracelets in for inclusion in the purification ceremony.

A member who owned a bracelet was instructed by an officer as to how it was to be used and taken care of, and the officer also made known to him the rigid penalties for violations of any part of the rules that govern the society.

WRIST CHARM OF
THE DEER SOCIETY

The exact wording of the instructions are society secrets known only to men who became members. How the charms worked is not known, but the bracelets were supposed to make it easier for a hunter to procure meat of the deer family, excluding the larger species such as the elk and moose.

Whatever the secret was, it is said that a member of the Deer Society was more apt to come home from a hunting trip laden with deer meat and be warmly welcomed by his wife than a non-member.

WARRIOR WEARING
DEER SOCIETY
COSTUME

Story of Fast Runner

A FAMOUS HUNTING STORY IS TOLD by the old man named Cloud, also called Cree. He describes what is considered one of the most outstanding feats in the history of the tribe.

"When I was about twenty-four years old I joined a group of young men who were going on a visit to other bands near the Fort Belknap Agency. There were ten or twelve in the party and all on foot.

We traveled by easy stages as there was no occasion to hurry our journey. We killed game for our needs as we moved from one camping place to another.

"As we passed the Big Lake (Lake Bowdoin) someone called our attention to some antelope that were at a distance. Presently, a buck left the band and came toward us in a reluctant mood, yet curious, perhaps, as we were all dressed in white and grey clothing and looked nearly alike. From a distance, we, too, may have looked much like a band of antelope.

"It was in the time when the juneberries were ripe (July) and the afternoon was very hot. Only in jest, I said to them, 'I am going to chase him if someone will carry my clothes and bundle.'"A man named Medicine Walk offered to carry my belongings, so I stripped off my clothing and wore only my moccasins and clout. My knife was in my belt. Still in jest, I made a play at 'making medicine' by taking soft sage with which I rubbed my legs and feet.

"At my approach the buck turned and ran back in a stiff-legged fashion, but still hesitated occasionally until I was rather close to him. The buck seemed to draw me on in the chase. He kept just so far ahead and finally dropped out of slight over a knoll. I speeded up and as I went over the hill, he was so close that I gave chase in earnest.

"As you see me now, I am well over six feet and I was always classed among the good runners. I never rode horseback, but traveled about on foot. The old men used to say to me, 'If you wish to keep on being a fast runner, you should not ride horses, as your legs will be bowed and your joints will grow fast together.'

"As we had subsisted on small and feathered game since we left home, the sight of antelope meat sent a gnawing desire for it through my system.

"I must have been made to run on and on as I did. I gave several war cries. I spoke aloud to the buck, 'You are not the only one on this land that can run. Begone. I am coming and I have a knife.'

"To my surprise, I gained right up to the bewildered animal. His mouth was open and, as he glanced back, he gave a muffled cry that sounded like he was winded and distressed. I was so close that I reached out and seized a hold near the hip. He broke away with the result that I lost ground. But again I was soon alongside of him. I caught hold of one of his horns and as he lunged forward he almost jerked me out of pace. In an instant my knife was out. I slashed his flank and immediately slackened my pace. He ran a short distance, then fell among the tall grass.

"I stopped and looked back. The party was not in sight. Soon two came running up and one of them was Medicine Walk. 'Why didn't you stop a long time ago?' he said. `It is so hot that you could burn your lungs up by so foolish a chase.' I said, 'Over in the tall grass lies your meat.'

There was a surprised look in their faces when as one they said, 'Did you say you killed?'

'The rest of the party came then and while I rested the others skinned the buck. I said to them, 'Skin him very carefully to see if he is a cripple, he may have had a broken limb some time.' But as we looked him over, the animal was as sound as could be.

"The distance that I ran was, as you call it now, about a mile and a half. The feat has always been a mystery to me. Up to that time I had no knowledge of herbs, which in later years were used by runners. My only thought is that it was very hot that day and the animal, fast as he was, perhaps was scared and winded."

Hunting Deer

MOOSE, ELK, DEER, AND ANTELOPE—among the larger game animals—were not hunted as extensively as the buffalo. They were hunted mostly in winter when they could be tracked.

After roaming the prairie from early spring until late in the fall, the tribe, when winter came, camped along the large heavily wooded rivers where there was fuel and shelter. Occasionally there was a buffalo hunt when buffaloes were found near camp. But usually the people had plenty of dried buffalo meat and tallow packed away so the hunters devoted themselves to the pursuit of smaller game for fresh meat.

"WHEN WINTER CAME THEY HUNTED FOR THE WHITETAILED DEER."

They watched for the whitetailed deer, which browsed about during the night and towards morning looked for a bedground in this way:

When the deer had decided to bed down it was its habit to first double back on its tracks for some distance, then make several broad jumps to one side and land with its four feet held closely together. It traveled a short distance then bedded down.

When a hunter saw that the tracks had doubled back, he made a large circle around the supposed bedground. If no tracks were found when the circle was completed, the deer was sure to be somewhere within its circumference. The hunter continued to circle around the bedground and kept a close lookout for the deer. Each time the circle was made smaller until the deer was spied and killed.

It is said that several whitetailed deer could be killed, one at a time in the same bedground providing the hunter continued to circle the place after each shot. If there was more than one deer there the rest seemed to become paralyzed in the bedground.

During the summer hunters hid near watering places and deer were killed in the evening when they came to drink.

Some hunters used a device to call the deer. It was made of thick bark, shaped like a boat, pointed at one end and cut square on the other. The piece was about one inch by two and three-fourth inches thick. It was hollowed out with the square end taken out so that it was like a shell when finished. A piece of very thin gristle or membrane pressed and dried was cut to fit over the entire top of the shell. A band of wet sinew was wrapped around the middle to hold the two parts together and allowed to dry. The device was placed halfway in the mouth, point first, and with both hands cupped over it was blown twice for each call. It sounded something like *woo-wa, woo* as in wood, *wa* as in warp.

During the full moon the hunter sat in a thicket. He called twice and waited for an answer. If a doe was near enough to hear the call it usually answered, at the same time coming nearer by several broad jumps. At each stop the deer waited for the hunter to call before it answered and came closer. Finally, when the deer was brought close enough to be seen and was within range, it was shot.

PART V

CEREMONIES AND SOCIETIES

Social and Secret Organizations

Women's Dances

The Grass Dance

Medicine Lodge Dance

Social and Secret Organizations

BEFORE THE ASSINIBOINE MADE PEACE with other tribes, they had very few social dances where men and women attended together. By the time the white man came, there were many kinds of dances which had been introduced by other tribes. To the uninformed, no foreign custom or color would be noticed in the dances. But the people of the tribe could readily identify these.

For example the Grass Dance, which is the main social dance today, was of Sioux origin; but the *Tancowaci*, or Dance Without Robes, originated among the Assiniboine women about the same time.

"Almost seventy winters ago," Red Feather relates, "I was one of a delegation that bought the Grass Dance from the Sioux. We went to their camp in a group and offered three horses and many goods. They accepted the offer

BOYS "ACT LIKE DOGS" SOCIETY
"BOYS HAD ORGANIZATIONS IMITATING THE WARRIORS' SOCIETIES ... THE 'ACT LIKE DOGS' HAD NO COUNTERPART IN THE OLDER MEN'S SOCIETIES."

and we came back. Their officers came abreast, singing, and joined our group, after which they taught us the songs and the ceremony from start to finish." This dance, the costumes worn, interpretation, and everything else about it, is described in detail in a chapter which follows.

Men had social organizations in which only males were permitted to join. Of those, known to be of Assiniboine origin, only a few are remembered by the very oldest people. These include the Kit Foxes, Big Dogs, Small Dogs, Ducks, Cranes, *Gakoges* (meaning Scrapes), *Gakemeze* (Stripes) and Soldiers.

The Gakoge were all young men from well-to-do families and their parades were very colorful. They dressed in elaborate costumes and met in large decorated guest lodges. No shiftless ones belonged to that society.

The different men's societies carried on their activities in the lodges of the officers. Small hand-drums were used and each society had different shaped rattles. Aside from the fact that each society had definite songs and dances, little is known about the societies, as their ceremonies were extremely secret.

ORNAMENTAL HEADPIECE
WORN BY MEMBERS OF THE
SECRET KIT FOX SOCIETY

Boys had organizations generally imitating the warriors' societies. Some of their groups, such as the "Act Like Dogs," had no counterpart in the older men's societies.

In this, the boys would go to the woods or in a ravine outside of camp and smear their bodies with white clay. They wore just clouts and moccasins. When properly decorated they would then sneak up near the edge of the encampment and, at a given signal, scatter and run into camp. The "Act Like Dogs" group snatched choice pieces of meat which had been hung up to dry, barking and growling all the while. To add to the realism, it was customary for women to run after the "Dogs" with sticks and in a playful manner harass them. Sometimes the women threw pieces of meat at them as they would to their own dogs. When each youth had enough meat the group went back to the woods, washed in a nearby creek or spring, cooked the meat at a campfire, feasted and discussed their adventure.

In the old days Assiniboine women did not enjoy social activities like the men. When men's meetings were in progress they were always too busy preparing the food used by the men. All routine work about the camp also fell to their lot and, so, there was very little time for the social ceremonies which are now practiced.

Women's Dances

THE *TANCOWACI*, DANCE WITHOUT ROBES, originated among the Assiniboine about the time Montana was made a Territory of the United States. It was first organized in the camp of the Hudesabina (Red Bottom Band) and later spread to other bands. It is classed as a woman's organization, the officers being old women. Men, however, may join in this dance.

The four women head officers hold the same rank. There are two Whippers, as in the women's Circle Dance, who are also officers holding lesser positions. The organization is composed only of these six positions.

The regular Camp Crier announces the place where the affair is to take place. As the organization was started before there were any large dance halls, it is usually held in the largest lodge owned by one of the four officers.

The Singers are men who volunteer. They use small drums, about a foot in diameter, made of rawhide stretched over a circular wooden framework. Each of the four Singers is provided with a drum. The Singers may change with each dance period if they wish.

When the Singers begin a song the four head women are the first to rise and dance to the first song period. Then the two Whippers join them, making another round. After this the Whippers raise their whips and point them

THE FEMALE ELK DANCE

toward the women dancers who then join the circle. After the women dance for a time and the circle becomes larger men join in by pushing their way into the circle beside the one they wish to dance with, or between two women whom they are accustomed to dancing with. Certain men and women call each other "dance partners," or Ones Who Dance Together Often.

As women head this dance they are the first to choose male partners. This they do by going over and pressing the toe of the man whom they wish to dance with.

There are no set rules to follow in the *Tancowaci* except for the principal part known as the "Take Down the Feathered Bonnet Song." Then the dance has been in progress for some time, this song is begun, whereupon four warriors who are asked by one of the women leaders, come forward and dance around within the circle, single file.

Four feathered bonnets, borrowed from the men dancers, are hung in a row in the back part of the lodge. When the four warriors dance past the bonnets they extend their arms reverently toward them. At the end of the fourth song period, they stop in front of the row and each man takes down a bonnet. Then the singers stop. The first warrior steps to the center of the circle and relates a war deed, holding the bonnet in his right hand. After this he puts the bonnet on the woman officer who is leading the circle. The other three warriors follow suit. As each one tells a war exploit he places his bonnet on the head of a woman officer.

When the warriors are through conferring the bonnets on the four women leaders, the same song is sung and all dance with the four officers wearing the bonnets. As the song ends the four women officers put their bonnets on the next four dancers to the right of them, the circle being completed by that time. This continues until the bonnets make the round of the dance circle, always being passed on to the left.

Ceremonial Drum

Before the next song is sung the four officers give articles away as an expression of gratitude for being honored with the bonnets. While this is being done the next four dancers stand in their places wearing the bonnets. At the end of each song period, the four bonnets are passed to the next four and always, during this intermission, the four who have worn the bonnets give things away. Everyone dancing in the circle is obliged to do this. If a man dancer already has a headdress on (which is fastened securely to his head) he merely holds the bonnet in front of him while performing and passes it to the next person at the end of the song period and then gives something away. No one is overlooked. When everyone dancing has been honored with a bonnet the dance ends and the bonnets are then returned to the owners. While the Bonnet Dance is in progress no one is allowed to leave the circle because frequently when some people see that a dance is going to be a Bonnet Dance they attempt to stay out of it.

The Bonnet Dance is not always performed at every *Tancowaci*, but generally only when there are a number of visitors from other bands or tribes present whom they wish to give things to. Sometimes if no visitors are present and the dance has not been performed for some time it is danced anyhow. Then the dancers either give gifts to each other or for the benefit of the whole dance group.

Tancowaci terminates much like the Grass Dance. A warrior re-enacts a war deed, such as when he charged an enemy line successfully. With a red-feathered ornament representing his weapon, he charges the entrance and emerges, followed by the crowd.

The only old time dance, other than religious, where women joined, was on the return of a war party. On these occasions the old women blackened their faces all over, the younger ones blackened each cheek, and, with the men painted the same, all danced together.

In this performance the women held objects or scalps of the enemy as they danced. It was considered an act of revenge for the relative who, in almost every family, had been killed by the enemy at some time.

But the most noted dance for women was a part of the ritual of the Female Elk Society, a religious organization.

When a band camped near a wooded creek, the women of this society went into the timber and changed their garments to short dresses with short sleeves. Then they would smear their exposed legs from the knees down and their arms to the elbows, with white clay. Headdresses of leaves were placed over their hair. An older woman, who was the Medicine Woman, led the group in which young women and girls were considered as young female elk, with the older women representing older female elk.

Two men, as bull elk, with wooden horns fastened to their heads, stayed far behind the females and danced, blowing on whistles at frequent intervals. They never joined the group of women but always kept far in the rear.

As the parade passed within the camp circle it was customary for warriors to join it. They would walk on each side and shoot arrows at the "Female Elk," being careful not to hit any of them. When an arrow fell among them, the group ran and scattered just as a herd of elk would do.

After a parade completed the camp circle, they returned to the woods and changed their costumes. The Female Elk Dance was then over until the same time a year later.

CEREMONY FOR A SUCCESSFUL HUNT.

The Grass Dance

NEARLY ALL LEADERS OF THE OLD TIME ASSINIBOINE SOCIETIES, both social and religious, have died during the past decade. Consequently, few social dances are now performed. By persistence, the preceding accounts were obtained from the few Old Ones still living; most of them had passed at least four score winters when interviewed in 1939 and 1940.

Because the principal dance still performed by the tribe is the Grass Dance, which as previously related by Red Feather was bought from the Sioux after the coming of the white man, it is described here in what is believed to be the most detailed account ever printed. All tribes in this area have since adopted this dance. Each tribe has added its own particular rites (usually of a social nature) to the performance.

Considerably changed from the original Sioux version, the Grass Dance of the Assiniboine is now composed of many social parts; but if the crowd is large and a pail of dog meat brought, it always concludes with the religious dance which originally ended the affair.

Of the origin of the dance it is told that a member of the Sioux tribe had a vision in which he was carried up to a spacious lodge. When he entered, the lodge was empty, except for a very large white rooster. The rooster said to him, "Sit down, my grandchild, I have sent for you because I want to instruct you in a new dance which you will carry back to your people and it will be the leading dance among the Indians. It will spread to other tribes but the name will always be known as the Grass Dance.

"As you know, the different dances among our people are fast dying out on account of the old leaders passing on. Some of those leaders were Medicine Men and passed away without instructing others to take their places. Also, the White Man is bringing new things for your young people in the way of amusements which are sometimes more appealing to them than your dances; so it is time now that your people adopt my dance."

The man was then instructed how to perform and dress for the dance.

For many years the Grass Dance was conducted only by men. Later, women were permitted to participate. Now everyone joins in up to the concluding parts, when only the officers may participate.

The grass dancer has always been a young man, slender, well built, fast

on his feet and able to perform the acrobatic movements which are a principal feature of the dance. Some of the songs are tuned only for fast dancers who sing while dancing to provide an exciting show for the spectators.

At first, it is told, the costume was made almost entirely of long slough grass. The neckpiece, arm, leg and ankle bands, a large belt with tailpieces to imitate the tail of the rooster and all other pieces of the costume, were grass.

As time passed, feathers, beads, trinkets, belts, mirrors and finally full buckskin dress suits with feathered or weasel-skin bonnets have been added. The principle of the costume has remained the same, except that grass has been largely replaced by other materials.

In general, dress for the occasion now varies according to the tasks of the participant. There is no rule governing the wearing of a costume.

Each man or woman may wear what is felt will best attract the attention of others. This is considered an appropriate place to exhibit the handiwork of different costumes; decorations on clothing denoting war achievements of the owner, or costumes obtained from other tribes.

Sometimes a dress or article may be worn by a woman to show that she has some act worthy of attention. A woman wearing a necklace of empty spools signifies that she has given away many articles made by sewing. Another dances with a long stick on which are painted colored stripes indicating the number of times she has made feasts in honor of dead relatives. A man may dance with a long stick, with cutout cardboard images of horses tied to showing the number of horses he has given away. Another may attach single eagle tailfeathers, each representing war bonnets given away. These outward signs of achievements were added to the Grass Dance by the Assiniboine.

Men fortunate enough to possess one, now dress in the present-day costume common to all celebrations—the full buckskin suit. A bonnet made of eagle tailfeathers or of white weasel skins with buffalo or steer horns is worn for a headdress. A shirt or coat of buckskin, either beaded or decorated by quillwork, with very long fringes on the sleeves and short ones across the back, is considered a correct dress coat; although a few wear all-beaded vests over a muslin shirt with long sleeves.

Present-day leggings are also of buckskin with wide bead or quillwork down the outside seams and long fringes back of the decorations. The loin cloths today are usually of dark blue flannel with a white border. Some are decorated by ribbons sewed in variegated colors on the seams. Beaded moccasins are worn.

In an older type of costume the tail of a whitetail deer was used for the headdress, made to resemble the double comb of a rooster. The hair was first clipped closely to resemble a hair brush. Then the stiff, long top hairs of the porcupine were woven butt-end first into the outer edge of the tailpiece. Several rows with bristles four or five inches long were thus woven in to create a wide-top headdress. The center of the head-dress, where the hair is clipped short, was dyed in many colors. Sometimes the downy piece of a

GRASS DANCER
IN FULL COSTUME

feather was attached to the tip of the rib. The butt was then fastened securely to the center of the headgear in such a way as to stand upright. A whole feather sometimes was used.

A tanned otter skin with the fur intact was split down the center so as to form a neckpiece, a good portion of which hung bib-like in front. Later, small round mirrors were used. They were fastened about three inches apart on each side of the split center of the neckpiece. When the dancer performed the mirrors reflected in the sun. Some young men, while sitting down, still reflect these mirrors toward young women whom they wish to attract. Frequently courtship results. Larger mirrors fastened to the center of carved flat pieces of wood have been carried in recent years.

Sometimes now tanned skins of kit foxes, with the fur intact, are used for neckpieces. They may be worn like the otter skin or around the neck, with the bushy tail down the back.

The few remaining very old men try to dress in a manner becoming their age and indicating the reputation they may have had in past war achievements. One who owns a full dress buckskin suit and eagle tailfeather headdress wears such a costume. Another may wear such a suit but on his head only a lone eagle tailfeather tied slightly back on top of the head with the tip hanging down the back. Now and then an old one may imitate the Sioux tribe by sticking the feather into the hair in the back or just to the side of the head in an upright position with the tip above the top of the head. Some old men wear the leggings made of dark blue woolen material, with beadwork below the knees, and a white cotton store shirt. Some

HEADDRESS OF A GRASS DANCER

decorate their white shirts with red paint, showing picture stories of war achievements. A red dot or dots show locations of wounds, sometimes with extra red splashes below the dots to indicate a serious wound. Sometimes an old man will place the location of a wound right over his heart.

It is told that one who did this was called to account right in the dance circle by one of his brothers-in-law, the only relatives allowed to openly challenge a performer. In cases like this the brother-in-law, after a satisfactory explanation has been made for the location of the wound mark, must give some object away, telling the recipient to take the object and shake hands with his brother-in-law, the performer. This challenge is usually made in good humor.

Bashful dancers sometimes dance with large feather fans, which they hold in front of their faces when dancing with women in the Women's Circle Dance. Such fans are made of tailfeathers from large birds, placed with the butts to the center and laced together into a circular shape. Usually a small round mirror is placed in the center of the fan. By holding the fan before his face the dancer can see his reflection in the glass making it unnecessary to look at anyone else. Sometimes these round fans are attached to the ends of fur ropes, made of otter skin wrapped on a stout cord, and hung down the back. One end forms the neckpiece while the fan on the other end drops down even with the hips.

Of late years some dancers have worn thin, tight-fitting long underwear beneath their regalia. With such a covering, other ornaments, such as tinsel, colored downy feathers and stars cut out of silver and gold paper can be sewed to the clothing. If underwear is not worn the body and limbs are painted in colors. The face is painted more artistically than any other part and as a result of the different designs it is often difficult to identify a dancer.

When the concluding parts of the Grass Dance are performed the following paraphernalia is used:

The all important feathered belt represents the tail of the rooster.

Eagle feathers sewed on an oblong piece of blue flannel covers the back of the legs from the hips down to the ground. Two long wing feathers stripped down to the ribs are attached to the top of the feathered cloth and are spaced about a foot apart. The ribs are covered with colored quillwork. A string of very small brass bells is tied to each tip and then looped down to the butt ends where they are fastened. A cloth belt completes this costume.

When the belt is worn the feathered backpiece drops down to the ground and the decorated ribs extend out from the back like a rooster's tail. Seven different belts, each worn by an officer, are used during a dance.

If a child holds an office, such as the *Waci-in-tancan* (Dance Leader), he is dressed like the older men.

For personal effects dancers may carry whatever they choose: a stone club with a decorated handle; stone or metal pipes and hatchets; or a ceremonial pipe kept in a buckskin sack the length of the pipe, with long sweeping fringes and bead or quillwork around the lower part of the bag. To this a long stick with a row of eagle tailfeathers, set close together as on a bonnet, may be attached. This is held upright during the ceremony.

In older days, warriors danced holding coup sticks, war hatchets, war pipes, pipes that had been taken on war party journeys, guns, small bows and arrows and other articles used in warfare. They carried such articles in order to be prepared, if called upon, to relate or re-enact war exploits.

Dancers' arm bands usually are of metal or tanned deer hoof skins with the two hoof buttons left on each band for ornaments. Round or widemouthed bells riveted to straps, are fastened securely around the legs below the knees or at the ankle. Some fasten a string of the bells from the hips to the garters or ankles.

Large hoops made of willows, measuring almost three feet in diameter and wrapped with tanned skins, are held in each hand when dancing.

The hoops are used in performing acrobatic movements. Single hoops are sometimes used.

Two Servers use a small forked spit made of willow which is covered with colored beads or quills. Only one spit is used and it is carried by the leader; the other Server is an assistant. A large forked spit, also made of willow and elaborately embellished with downy feathers, beads and quills, is used by a lone dancer, one of the young grass dancers. This is the only part necessarily filled by a young man because it requires very fast and fancy dancing.

The Spoon Keeper is another one-man part filled, usually, by a middle-aged man. The spoon is made of the outside shell of a buffalo horn with a wooden handle decorated with beads or quills. The Spoon Song is not tuned as fast or as long as the Forked Spit Song.

The dance requires two Whippers, who sit to one side of the entrance. Their whipstocks are made of wood, with lashes attached to the ends. The wooden whipstock is about four inches wide. One edge is notched with points like saw teeth. A tanned kit-fox skin with the fur and tail intact is attached by the nose of the skin to the top of the stock so that the stock and skin hang together only by this attachment. A wrist strap is provided for the convenience of the Keeper.

It is told that in the early days of the Grass Dance if some officer was unruly in the hall one of the Whippers made him kneel in the center and the other sawed the back of his neck with the notched side of the whipstock edge. As a punishment it caused much pain but did not draw blood.

The Keeper Of The Drum has charge of the drum. He keeps it at his home, sees to its care, and is required to bring it personally to each dance. In using the drum, four stakes are driven into the ground to form a square. The drum is hung inside and off the ground by tying it to these stakes, which are wrapped with colored beads. The tips, which project about a foot above the top of the drum, are decorated with dyed horse tail in different colors. The vibration of the drum when beaten keeps the tail ornaments fluttering, which adds to the already colorful movement of the group in the center of the dance hall.

Four decorated drum sticks in the care of the Song Leader are used. The knobs are covered with beaded buckskin and the handles are wrapped with different colored beads. Tailpieces are sometimes attached to the ends.

When the Singers take their places around the drum, the Song Leader presents a decorated drum stick to three visiting Singers from other tribes. If there are no visitors present he passes them to well-known Singers in the group. Singers are not always the same, as any good one may volunteer. As long as there is room around the drum any one may sit in. Singing is done sitting down.

Decorated drum sticks are not used throughout the performance because continuous use will ruin the colorful decorations in a short time. They are used only to show respect to a visiting Singer or a worthy local person. A substitute is used while the decorated one is held by the handle in the left hand and the closed hand held tightly against the left temple while the singing is in progress. All other Singers are provided with plain drum sticks. Some who are always present own their own drum sticks. Decorated drum sticks are used when an account of a war deed is being told. During the speaking the drum is hit several times at intervals as an applause.

The Keeper Of The Drum is not always one of the Singers. But may be one of the Dancers or even a spectator. Oftentimes the Drum Keeper is a child of a prominent family who sees to it that the drum is well taken care of. The child usually brings food for the Singers to each dance. The object in selecting a child as the Keeper Of The Drum is to promote teamwork.

AT A PREVIOUS DANCE THE DATE for the next one is set. When the day arrives, the Camp Crier announces it and calls the officers to the dance hall. The hall, in summer, is a circular enclosure without a roof. Green cottonwoods with branches and leaves intact are placed upright in holes in the ground and tramped in, with the entrance to the south. In winter a large circular frame structure with shingled roof, built for the purpose, is used.

Usually the day before a dance, the Crier visits the lodge of each officer and takes an object which the owner values highly. These are deposited in the hall, to be reclaimed upon the attendance of the owner at the dance. When objects are left unclaimed the Crier holds one at a time in full view and proclaims the name of the owner to the people. Then he destroys it.

With the dance about to begin the Camp Crier repeats the summons three more times just within the camp circle. At the conclusion of the last call, he goes to the hall and makes note of all the officers present. Late arrivals are placed in a group in the middle of hall as prisoners. He levies a fine on each one, then relatives come forward and pay a fine, usually in food, for release of the tardy officials. This is always done in good humor. The Crier keeps account of the fines and checks each one paid at the next performance and if any fines are not paid he announces the names of the delinquent persons, renews the fines and levies additional ones.

It is told that when the tribe first adopted the Grass Dance, harsh methods similar to those which governed the soldier were used to compel attendance of officers. In those days after the Crier had completed a fourth round of the camp circle, he went to the dance hall and checked the officers. If any were absent, this man accompanied by two soldiers went to the lodge of the absent one. If the officer was ill or if there was illness in the family he was excused, but if he gave a poor excuse one of the soldiers, standing in the doorway, shot the tardy officer in the stomach with a knobbed, padded arrow. If the officer immediately arose, took the arrow and hurried forward, one shot was sufficient but if he was sullen he was shot with a second arrow, then allowed to remain in his lodge. It was very seldom that the second knobbed arrow had to be used as it was not padded.

The Drum Keeper and the Singers are always the first to reach the hall. This makes it possible to go over any new songs they are learning. The drum is first tightened, then it is gently tapped and the songs are sung in a low tone of voice. As the participants arrive the songs are sung louder and the beat of the drum increases. During this time songs are sung at random, principally to arouse the crowd. Dancers who arrive early may begin dancing if they wish.

Young Grass Dancer with forked spit

As in other dances and ceremonies, rules and regulations governing the Grass Dance are strictly followed. Each person or group responsible for a part must do the part to perfection. Other persons not in the group observe the performance closely for any errors. If a part is left out or not done properly, officials of that dance group are fined. For example, if the Song Leader begins with the wrong song and his group follows, he and his group are fined for the error. But if the Singers do not follow the Song Leader, he is the only one fined.

All dancing by both men and women before the concluding part of the Grass Dance is composed of social steps. During this time announcements by different parties can be made. Anyone wishing to make an announcement must do so through the official announcer who is available at all times without pay. But he does not refuse a small gift or money offered to him.

The Announcer and Interpreter is an important person. He is well dressed, possesses a fine voice and is gifted with a command of language which at times is intermingled with good jokes, much to the amusement of the crowd. He can be sarcastic at times, but usually this is more humorous than caustic. For instance, if someone is receiving a gift and the recipient is slow in coming forward, he might say, "Why do you rise so slowly, jump up and run over here, this gift is something you have been wishing for for a long time."

If the Announcer is busy listening to someone making known to him in a low voice what he is to proclaim, another person who wishes to make an announcement may get another to do it. This is allowed when the regular official is busy. The announcements are usually gifts and donations to the poor, to visitors, or to different dance groups. The last represents food for the next affair. Chattels given to the dance groups are sold at auction and the money is spent for expenses incurred in the upkeep of the hall. These donations are made in honor of relatives or children, or in payment of fines.

In recent years when tribal officials desire to raise funds in large amounts for some cause they give a list of names to the Song Leader who, with his group, then sings Brave Heart Songs for the prominent people or the children of families listed. The person whose name is announced must then dance. After the first verse, relatives and close friends come forward and also dance. After the second verse all the male dancers join in to the end of the song. After that the person and his relatives and friends, through the announcer, give things away. Sometimes, the donations run into such things as horses, harness, buggies, guns, buckskin clothing, cattle, saddles or money.

A family who has lost a dear one, saves food, clothing, money and many other trinkets for as long as a year and then takes all this to a dance to give away in honor of the departed. The family usually requests first that a song be sung with the name of the deceased worked into the song.

After male dancers have danced for sometime, one of the two men who head the Women's Circle Dance requests through the announcer that the women be given a chance to dance. The announcer then makes the request in the following words: "The Circle Dance leader said, 'It is time to admire the women as they dance alone.' Let them dance by all means."

Women have their own drum, which is slightly smaller than the men's. They also have their Drum Keeper, who is a child or an adult. Because the Women's Circle Dance is an added feature of the Grass Dance proper, paraphernalia used is limited to a drum, four staffs and two whips.

Two staffs with crooks are carried by the dance leaders. They are fully explained in the previous chapter, "Dances and Social Gatherings." The other two staffs are without a crook and wrapped with wide strips of tanned dog skin with the hair, always of black or dark brown color, intact. Two eagle tailfeathers are tied to the tip and sharpened at the butt. The staffs are shouldered when dancing. The second Staff Bearer rates next in position to the first Bearer.

The two Whip Keepers dance next to the Staff Bearers, being the seventh and eighth in line. Two older men, who have some war experience, head the women dancers. The whips are of long limber willows, painted in different colors or with some bark left intact as an ornament. In later years buggy whips were substituted for these.

Singers for the women are the regular Singers, dancers and spectators, as anyone can come forward to join in the singing if there is room around the drum. The drum is held up by the side straps and the singers stand throughout the period of dancing.

When the first song is started, the two men immediately take their places and the Staff Bearers and Whip Keepers join in. These eight dance for a time and then other women, who are dressed to dance, come forward. After that anyone may join.

If the women are slow in joining, the Whip Keepers raise their whips towards them to hurry them forward. Now and then, one who is a sister-in-law of one of the Whip Keepers may harass her by keeping her seat. Then the Whip Keeper hurries over and gives her a few taps on the shoulder, or stays there with the whip poised until she stands up. This, too, is done in good humor to amuse the crowd.

As the dancers join and the circle is completed, another circle can be started within.

The Circle Dance is danced, moving toward the left, raising one foot slightly off the floor followed by the other. Once in awhile, instead of the Circle Dance, the announcer instructs the Singers to sing the Night Dance Song in which the performers dance without moving from their places. A circle is not usually formed. Instead each couple or trio dance scattered about the hall. The trio represents a man with two women partners or a woman between two men.

The Night Dance for men and women, which is of Assiniboine origin, is performed at times during the Grass Dance. The stationary position of the dancers is due to the fact that small dance lodges in the early days before large halls were built precluded more movement.

The Night Dance Song is of a sentimental nature. As the dance progresses couples dance closer and closer together. Husbands and wives of a jealous nature resent this. So frequently when the Night Dance is announced such ones bid their mates to dance with them alone.

After the women have danced for a time, the male grass dancers may join in merely by getting into the circle beside the one they wish to dance with. The men put their arms over the shoulders of their partners and hold them around the waist. If a man is dancing with a woman on each side of him, he places an arm over each one, while the women both hold him around the waist.

Women choose their partners by going over to where a man is sitting. If they press the man's toe with theirs, the man then rises and they go forward to find a place in the circle.

Sometimes two women will bid a brother-in-law to dance with them and, usually to tease them, he refuses. Then they take hold, one on each arm, and drag him forward. Sometimes if the man resists the women will deliberately drag him across the floor, to the amusement of the spectators.

The women's dance is very long as it takes time to form a complete circle.

Spectators usually join in the dance, either voluntarily or when some dancer comes and asks them to dance. There is a rest period between songs. If someone wishes to make an announcement it can be done at this time while the dancers remain standing in their places.

The dance ends without much ado, the Singers merely strike the drum with several hard blows when the dancers have had enough. On account of the length of time consumed by each Circle Dance, they are performed only once or twice during a Grass Dance.

LIKE SOME OF THE MEN'S COSTUMES the women's dresses are decorated with silk ribbons in different colors, usually sewed around the skirt from the waist down to the hem, and around the edges of the roomy sleeves. Some beaded leggings are worn. High-topped, beaded or quillwork moccasins are worn without the leggings, the high top serving this purpose. The neck band, which reaches halfway to the waist on some dresses, is decorated with small sea shells. Elk teeth dresses nowadays are rare. A few buckskin dresses elaborately embellished with bead or quillwork, with fringes, are still worn by young women. Any girls who join regularly in the Circle Dance are dressed like older women.

Throughout the dance, it will be noted, great responsibility is placed on the Song Leader. He must learn all of the songs and be able to lead them in order. The dancers are guided by the songs so it is not often that they commit an error, but the Song Leader is more liable to commence the wrong number and be fined for the error.

If a part of a dancer's dress, such as a loose bell, feather or other ornament, falls to the floor while a men's dance is in progress the owner is not allowed to pick it up. As soon as the fallen part is noticed by the dancers they commence to dance around it, forming a group. As the group becomes larger with most of the dancers joining, the Singers change to a war chant and beat. When this chant is sung all of the dancers circle the object with the old warriors inside of the circle near the fallen ornament. The object represents an enemy and after a time one of the warriors picks it up and the singing and dancing ceases. With the object in his right hand he points it in the direction he once journeyed with a war party and relates a war story, after which he hands it back to the owner who comes to the center of the circle and, through the announcer, gives something to the relator or to the dance group.

When the general dancing has continued past the middle of an afternoon or, if at night, past midnight, the concluding parts of the Grass Dance are then performed. Up to that time no eating is allowed. If anyone is found eating, except children, the person is seated in the center of the dance circle and told to consume a large pail of some kind of soup. Because it is an impossible amount, relatives usually come forward and ask to pay a fine to have the party released.

Anytime during the dance if the Singers wish to rest they sing the Smoking Song. A request is worded in the song which indicates the desire to smoke. The Drum Keeper sits in the back of the hall with a ceremonial pipe and a large supply of tobacco. Now and then he fills the pipe, lights it, and passes it to the officers. When the Smoking Song is sung, he is the first to approach the Singers with a filled pipe. After that, others may come forward and offer pipes to them. Then the song stops and everyone who wishes to may smoke.

Just before the concluding parts, the Dance To The Ten Songs is sung by the Singers in which everyone attending is obliged to join in. Spectators and the very old people always stand in their places and keep time to the beat of the drum by slightly bending the knees. Everybody is required to dance or stand as the Ten Songs are sung. A fine is levied on those who remain sitting. Those disabled or not well are allowed to keep their seats if they wish.

The two Whippers, who are also officers, are always the first to rise to all men's dance songs. They sit together to one side of the entrance, opposite the two Servers, and upon rising they separate; one going to the right and the other to the left, dancing along in front of the seated dancers and meeting in the back of the dance circle. From there they dance side by side to the center and separate, mingling with the dancers, wending their way to their seats where they remain dancing until a song ends.

The only duty required of the Whippers is to see that all male dancers who are able will dance at each song and dance period. If any dancer is still seated after they meet, the Whipper comes back to learn why the dancer remains seated. Sometimes, the one making the round to the right, holds the whip poised threateningly, causing dancers to begin rising long before he gets to them. These officers desire a large number on the floor in order to make a dance successful. If the Singers sing a fast one for the young dancers, the Whippers do not rise but all who can dance to the song are obliged to join. In the early days of the Grass Dance, Army cavalry swords were used. Finally whips, as described, came into use.

When the Ten Song Dance commences the Whippers get all who are able to their feet. The people dance with much enthusiasm during the long period, but toward the end, if they show any signs of slowing down, a man blows a bone whistle vigorously to arouse the dancers. He keeps this up to the end of the period.

The concluding parts of the Grass Dance then follow, with the male Singers chanting the Take Down The Feathered Belt Song, assisted by two women seated nearby. These women are well-known Singers. They finish the chorus or last part of a song, which is sung without words. When their part comes, the men stop singing and beating the drum. As result the high voices which blend together can be heard clearly above the jingling of the small bells which adorn the dancers. As the two female voices approach the end of the song the Drum Beaters and male Singers drown them out by commencing the next verse.

The two Servers, who sit to one side of the entrance commence to dance to the Belt Song. They start from their places and dance a complete round back to their stations with each song period. The belts, which are carefully bundled in muslin bags, are hung in a row in the back of the hall but within the circle of seated dancers. As the two pass the row of belts, with the Head Server in the lead, they raise their arms, palms toward the row of belts, a sign which indicates respect for the belts. These belts have the same significance as war bundles made by Medicine-Men Leaders of war parties for carrying on war journeys.

When the Grass Dance came into existence there was still warfare among the different tribes. When a person received a belt at a dance it was expected of him to accompany a war party the first chance he had and take the belt along as a war bundle to wear during any engagement with an enemy. For this reason, many refused to accept belts. They declined by giving away a valuable gift either to some individual or to the whole dance group.

When four verses of the Belt Song end, singing stops and the Servers each take down a bundle. They make a smoke offering with the piece of dried sweetgrass, tied to each drawstring, by laying it on live coals. Over the smoke offering the bundles are passed back and forth several times and unwrapped. The first two purified belts are placed side by side on a blanket spread under the row of bundles. Then each Server takes a Headman by the hand, and makes him kneel behind each belt. The two then face the entrance, kneeling. The Servers next girdle themselves with their purified belts. Then they give a belt to each of the following officers: The Big Spit Keeper, the Spoon Keeper and the belt with red-dyed feathers to a warrior who was wounded by an enemy. These officers remain seated, holding their belts in front of them.

Next a Server takes a pail containing cooked dog meat and places it in the center, while the other comes forward leading a warrior by the hand and seats him near the pail. This man represents an enemy and he is mentioned as the "Enemy" when any reference is made to him. He usually has a wooden gull painted red and a flock of horse mane, representing a scalp, tied near the mouth of the barrel. The Servers take their seats as they complete this part.

The Singers start the next song and the two kneeling officers rise on their knees and dance with their bodies swaying from side to side. At a part in the song where mention is made of the belt, the two extend their arms forward in supplication.

At the third verse they rise and, holding their belts in front of them, move forward, dancing to the left as they circle the hall. When they pass the entrance the two Servers rise and follow the two, all dancing single file to the back of the hall, the starting point, where the first two don their belts. As the last verse is sung and the file commences the last round, the Big Spit Keeper,

GRASS DANCE BELT CEREMONY

the Spoon Keeper and the one with the red-feathered belt, joins them, single file, in the order named.

When the seven dance past the Enemy, he maneuvers around behind the pail, pointing his gun at the rear warrior wearing the belt with red feathers. The belted warrior dodges the imaginary bullets fired by the Enemy who makes the shots by aiming the gun and with the right hand throws a handful of dry dirt, representing powder smoke.

As the last verse of the fourth song is ending, all seven are back to the starting point, maneuvering by dancing toward the Enemy. The Enemy shoots the rear warrior down and before he can count coup, one among the non-dancers rushes forward and rescues the wounded. The rescuer must be one who had earned the achievement and can re-enact it.

When the wounded one is assisted to his feet and led away the other six persons of his group file past the pail each tapping the rim as an act of counting coup. At the last man's tap the singing stops; the Enemy and the rescuer come to the center of the hall to relate where and how they had won the achievements they have re-enacted. With this conclusion, all sit down.

One of the Servers now walks over to take down the Big Spit from its place in the rear of the hall. He places it in the right hand of the Keeper. The Keeper grasps the spit just below the fork and the Server, holding the sharpened end, leads him to his station which is near the entrance in front of the seats of the Servers.

The Singers sing the Big Spit Keeper's Song. He sits quietly through the first verse, which is sung without words. At the second verse, when the words, "Arise, arise, 'they say' it means you, Big Spit Keeper," he slowly rises and dances gently around his place.

Because this is a solo part and the principal feature of the dance the crowd is tense. Absolute quiet prevails. Above the beat of the drum and the singing, the big and small bells which adorn the legs of the dancer, peal forth commanding the attention of all onlookers.

This part is always assigned to a young man who is an outstanding dancer, and can do rapid and fancy stepping with much body motion. The young man is generally single and in this part, he receives not only the attention of the crowd but of the maiden he most desires to charm. Chiefly for this reason the Big Spit Keeper does his utmost to perform his part skillfully. He can be fined if he makes a mistake but he is not afraid of the penalty for the chance to show his skill in front of so many and the possibility of winning the attention of his chosen maiden is worth the risk. After he wins a wife he can retire, as generally is done by most Big Spit Keepers.

As the song goes into the third verse the beat of the drum is increased and the singing becomes louder and more brisk. This arouses the dancer and he begins putting more energy into his movements. He dances toward the left moving along in front of where the women, spectators and dancers are seated. Through the fourth and last verse the tempo is the same. At the end of the song he is back at his station. Then singing stops; but to the beat of the drum the dancer continues for a short time.

Soon another song follows with more energy. This arouses the dancer and he puts even more life into his movements, dancing back and forth on the path he is to follow. He dances in this way throughout the first part of the song. By the beginning of the last half the singing and beat of the drum is very rapid. The dancer keeps time and moves toward the pail containing dog meat, holding the spit, point forward.

The pail of dog meat has been set in the place previously used by the belt keepers. As he passes the pail he almost touches it with the sharp point of the spit. He turns and dances at the same pace toward his station or starting point, going in a circle. Just before he reaches his station the song changes to the time of the first part, which is slower. This gives him time to get his wind for the next fast part.

The dancer makes three rounds dancing in this manner. In the fourth round, when he arrives at the pail, he sticks the spit into the pail and circles it several times ending the part with the spit left in the pail. The song ends as he concludes this last act, song and performance ending together. The dancer takes his seat. The crowd does not make a noisy applause but rather indicates its interest in this performance by being quiet and attentive.

Now the song leader and an assistant go to the pail to make an inspection. If the spit has pierced the dog's head every officer is obliged to give something away, but there are no war dances or telling of war exploits. If the dog's head is not touched, but the spit pierces another piece, the Head Server takes the spit with the piece of meat stuck to it and holds it up for the crowd to see. Then he calls the Song Leader over and standing opposite holds the spit above his head making him reach for the meat with his mouth. The Song Leader after several attempts finally bites it off the spit.

Then he goes to his seat and places the piece on his plate, as it is not yet time for anyone to eat.

The Server Song is sung and the two Servers dance with the Head Server in the lead holding the small spit in his right hand. They make a complete round past the pail of dog meat. As they pass, the leader holds the spit devoutly over the pail and the other follows suit by extending his right hand over it. They dance four rounds, always past the pail to their station at the end of each verse. The song and dancing stops at the end of the fourth verse and the Leader takes the pail from the center to the men's side. Then each Server selects two warriors from among the dancers and seat the four near the pail, after which, the leader dips up the dog meat, using the small spit, into plates placed before each one. The dog's head is included in the portion on the first plate. When each warrior is served the two take their seats.

The Singers sing the Spoon Keeper's Song to which that officer dances. He, too, makes four rounds; one round to each song verse. At the end of the last verse he is in front of the four seated warriors, where he stops.

With the tip of the spoon he touches the dog meat on the first plate and points it in the directions of the four principal winds; then offers it to the warrior, who, if his conduct the previous night and this day is beyond reproach, touches the tip of the spoon with his lips. This performance is repeated in front of the other three warriors and also for the Dance Leader and Song Leader. Those who think that they are not worthy to touch the sacred spoon refuse by turning their heads aside. The penalty for accepting the offering unworthily, it is believed, is to be bitten by a dog sometime afterward.

When the spoon offering is concluded the two Servers place pails of different foods in front of groups and one from each group helps serve. When the serving is well along, the Spoon Keeper proclaims to the crowd that "it is time to eat." Everyone who is served can then start eating.

Most white people believe that dog meat comes from a grown dog. Actually the meat used in the ceremonial part of the Grass Dance is from pups seven to ten weeks old. They are weaned early and fed on different soups until they go into the pot. The meat is then tender and fat. Old people usually have a number of well-fed pups on hand and sell them to others who promise to take part of the dog meat to a dance. This food is not eaten everyday nor used in a common way. Dog meat is present only at large feasts and religious gatherings. It is the principal food used when inviting a Medicine Men to administer to a sick one.

The dog meat is prepared as follows:

A tripod is set up and the pup, stunned by a blow, is hung by the neck until straight. When the animal is too light to strangle by its own weight, this is done by pulling downward by its hind legs. The dead pup is placed on a large blazing fire, built on the ground in the open.

In this way the hair is all singed off. After this the animal is laid to one side of the fire and scraped clean, singeing being repeated on spots not properly cleaned. The animal is then butchered, cleaned and cut up into pieces about three inches square. The pieces are washed and the skin is scraped in water until it is of a yellowish color. Several changes of water are used. Then the meat is placed in a kettle over the fire to boil, adding no seasoning until the required tenderness is obtained. It is then cooled and served cold.

At this stage of the Grass Dance a group of male spectators usually gets together and one goes into the dance circle and asks for food to distribute among the men and boys who are onlookers. The group always collects money among male spectators, giving it to the dance group in return for food. Sometimes, a big-hearted spectator promises a beef to the dance group, making his wish known through the official announcer. Women dancers serve the women spectators.

As the dancers are served first they are usually through eating before the last serving is done. The four Warriors, when finished, resume their seats after which the Head Server takes the dog's skull. Pointing with it to the four wind directions he lays it down in the center of the dance circle, a sign for the Singers to sing the War Dance Song.

During the singing, the servers seat four warriors other than the four who were previously fed. These four must be warriors who have war achievements—not one or two exploits that they can tell about but many. The people become tired of listening to the same old stories told again and again by one who has no others to tell about.

In relating war exploits, it is usually the custom to give proof, like naming someone still living who was in the war party. They must also give the location, the enemy tribe or a battle which is well known, and mentioned many times by different warriors who were in it.

Four warriors are brought forward for each pail of dog meat brought to the dance at this time. Eight warriors are eligible for the war dance if there are two pails of dog meat, and so on. When more than four are to participate, four out of the group can volunteer without being chosen by the Servers. This gives some warriors who like to tell of war deeds the chance to join the War Dance. It so happens, sometimes, that all of the warriors over four are brought forward but if there are visitors from other tribes present, there is no trouble in finding volunteers.

The warriors dance to the song four times around the skull to four verses. When the song ends the beat of the drum is continued; the singers merely keep time to the drum with a chant. Then the dancers commence their War Dance.

In this the skull is the enemy. Each dancer re-enacts some exploit directed toward that which he will relate near the conclusion of the War Dance. While the dance is in progress the crowd is at a high pitch with much conversation going on between parties discussing the re-enactments. Some among the spectators chant along with the Singers. Unlike the Big Spit Dance part, where the crowd is perfectly quiet, the War Dance is a noisy affair. The warriors' portrayal is usually so graphic that it holds the attention of the crowd to the end.

As each dancer completes his performance he steps back of the line, keeping time to the drum in a stationary position. All through the performance wives of the warriors keep up a continual applause in a high-pitched tone, much like the call of the guinea hen. The dance concludes with the last warrior completing his act.

The first in the line of dancers picks up the skull and points it in the direction he once journeyed with a war party, relating the account of his act. When finished he puts down the skull in its place on the floor. The Singers applaud by hitting several hard blows on the drum at each pause in the story. The same is done for each warrior speaking. The next in line goes through the same procedure, followed by the others to the last man. If any warrior thinks that his conduct in the past night or that day has made him unworthy, he does not pick up the skull but merely holds his right hand above it, pointing in the direction he traveled with a war party.

When all have related their various exploits the first warrior steps forward. Through the announcer he gives some object away. Then the others do the same. Usually wives and close relatives donate something in honor of the performers. It is regarded as unbecoming for a warrior to hold the attention of a crowd with his war story and not give something away afterward.

When all of the warriors, their wives and relatives have been heard and have finished giving things away, others who wish to make announcements or donations are then taken care of by the announcer.

At this time, too, newborn babies are announced and donations made in their honor. If there are visitors from other tribes present, they are given many objects at this time.

During this pause in the concluding parts of the Grass Dance, Brave Heart Songs are sung for the children of prominent families, who, after they have danced, gave things away. When all those who wish to give something away are done, the Singers begin the closing song in which all either rise and dance or stand in their respective places. No one is allowed to leave.

Of late years a Doorkeeper has been appointed. In a frame structure hall provided with a big door, he keeps the door locked from the time the concluding parts are started. If anyone has a good excuse to leave, the Doorkeeper allows it with the understanding that the one going out must come back and stay until it is over. Sick persons are allowed to go home at any time.

The closing song of the Grass Dance is sung four times. At the beginning of the fourth singing, the officer wearing the red-feathered belt, which signifies that the wearer was wounded in a battle by an enemy, dances forward into the center of the circle. Here he maneuvers about pointing the belt, which he has ungirded, in the direction of the doorway. As the song ends he rushes through the door making a path for the crowd which immediately follows. The closed door represents the enemy line and the officer, in ending the affair, re-enacts a war exploit where he rushed the enemy line successfully and his comrades followed. The dance ends.

Medicine Lodge Dance

IN THE OLD DAYS THE ANNUAL MEDICINE LODGE DANCE was a religious ceremony. It was the important event of the year—much as Christmas is to the white man except for the significance. All people looked forward to it and saved offerings for that time. A Medicine Man, as past master of all the rules which governed the dance, acted as Leader.

Today this ceremony is erroneously called "Sun Dance," according to Standing, seventy-nine-year-old Medicine Man who still leads the dance each year.

Nothing about the old time Medicine Lodge Dance was done in haphazard fashion as there were heavy penalties for all mistakes. Preparations were started as soon as the snow was gone, in order to be well prepared for the main ceremony which took place about the middle of June, in the Full Leaf Moon. If people of the tribe sponsored the dance they furnished everything that was used. If a head Medicine Man took the responsibility, as was often the case, he did the same.

MEDICINE LODGE DANCE

The first ceremonial song was sung in the early spring as soon as the offerings were collected. A certain number of different kinds of offerings had to be available for this first meeting. If the tribe moved about there was a gathering of the headmen of the dance at each new location. Three such special meetings took place before the fourth or final one.

The fourth song meeting ended at daylight. Then all Scouts, as men who had war records were known, were sent to some nearby stand of timber to select a Medicine Pole. A great crowd of people followed to see the Scouts re-enact their war deeds in the timber, after which offerings were made at the foot of the tree selected.

This done, the Scouts returned to camp with a branch of the tree which they presented to the Leader. He gathered all offerings together, then led the Scouts back to the tree. Standing at its foot he made offerings to the Thunder Bird; he then instructed two choppers to cut the tree down.

The two chopped with left-handed strokes around the trunk in the direction that the sun travels. All limbs were cut off, but some of the smaller branches with leaves were saved. A nest was built with these branches and placed in the fork of the tree at the very top. Short poles then were placed under the Medicine Pole and men, working in pairs, carried it to camp.

The procession which followed was a rare lark for young men and women who, on this day, were permitted to be openly together without a chaperon; but at the proper time they had to be in the long parade, dressed in their best clothes.

Sweethearts rode double on horses, using ornamented saddles and bridles. Each mounted couple dragged a pole by means of a rope tied to the saddle. This pole was later to be used at the dance lodge. Scouts sang war songs, the choruses of which were taken up by the women. Young couples joined in now and then but most of them were so interested in each other that the journey back to camp ended all too soon.

After reaching camp the ceremonial pole was carved down the sides in zigzag and straight lines to represent lightning. Other symbols were carved at the top beneath the nest. The Leader then directed the men in setting up the Medicine Pole and the lodge was finished by sundown. If several bands joined to participate in the dance, a double lodge was built to accommodate all who wished to attend.

After this the participants took places behind a breastwall made of chokecherry branches. The Leader started the dance by throwing an un-tanned buffalo hide, with a strip of hair left intact down the back, into the center of the lodge. This act indicated that the lives of the people depended on the meat of the buffalo.

The Singers, with long drum sticks, sat around the dry hide using it as a drum. A Medicine Man, who had been asked to do so by the Leader, led the singers with a rattle.

Young men who were candidates were coached by experienced Medicine Men and painted to represent their beliefs. Their faces and bodies were painted to the waist.

Both men dancers and the women, who were separated from the men by a curtain, had bone whistles in their months. During the dance they kept time with them. Since they prayed to the Thunder Bird, candidates were considered to be young Thunder Birds just hatched. The whistles imitated chirping.

It is told that very long ago sacrifices were made to the Double Faced Being, a war god. The men who joined asked for war favors in return for offerings and other sacrifices made to him. In later years all prayers and offerings were made to Thunder Bird, the God of Rain. As part of the

MEDICINE LODGE POLE PROCESSION

ceremony, men dancers pierced their breasts. Two thongs were looped through the slits and made secure. The other ends were brought together and tied to the top of the center pole. Then they swayed back and forth dancing on and on until they either fainted or went into a trance. It was believed that if fasting and sacrifices were in order, a favorable vision or some future war glory was seen while in the trance or faint.

Others pierced their backs near each shoulder blade. To these holes thongs also were attached. The other end was then tied to one or more buffalo skulls which were dragged around within the camp circle.

At the conclusion of sacrifice the men came into the lodge. The Master, with a prayer for each, then removed the thongs and hung them on the Medicine Pole. That was the end of the fast for these men and they could go home if they wished, even though the dance was not ended.

Some warriors were known to cut out pieces of their flesh and offer them to the War God in exchange for an enemy.

Prayers and offerings were made by the people each day of the ceremony. Some were in thanksgiving for past favors, while others asked for future benefits. At that time pledges were renewed by many.

Families, with either the man or the woman representing the household, offered sacrifices to the Thunder Bird for a safe journey through the summer and winter. In return for such a favor they promised a renewal of sacrifices at the next annual dance. Others promised to entertain the leaders of the Medicine Lodge Circle with a feast if they were successful in some war achievement.

Often a young man would join the dance because he had promised to do so if he won the affections of a young lady. Perhaps by that time they were married. If so, while the young husband danced, his wife came into the lodge and in his honor gave away things to needy persons.

A common pledge by families was the following: "Take pity on us, O Thunder Bird, we pray that you look this way; grant that we journey without sickness through the summer and that the snow falls on us. Allow us again to see green grass so we can make sacrifices to you."

Occasionally relatives who had been ill for a long time, were taken to the dance and the headman was asked to treat them. Usual treatment was to make water flow by magic from the Medicine Pole into a container. This was given to the sick one as a curative drink. This was one of the rare sights at a Medicine Lodge Dance. Only a Lodge Leader who had been given the power performed this act.

When the dance was about to end the Master instructed the Singers to count lodge poles and sing a song for each pole. All people joined in the dance, where they stood, until the songs were finished. Just before this last group of songs the Master prayed aloud, then offered to the Thunder Bird all the sacrifices of the people. He asked for a good rainy season which would bring prosperity to the people with an abundance of berries, root foods, and game.

The Medicine Lodge Dance lasted two nights and one and a half days with a rest period from each midnight till morning. It was a complete fast from beginning to end. When the dance was over at noon of the second day the people moved their entire camp to another location some distance away from the Medicine Lodge.

It is said that when a Medicine Lodge Dance was over a dark cloud usually came up in the west late that evening. This was followed by rain accompanied by much thunder and lightning. Then the people whispered one to another. "The Thunder Bird and his helpers are coming for the offerings."

THE STORY IS TOLD ABOUT THE YOUNGEST DAUGHTER of a chief of the Red Bottom Band who had been ill a long time. She was brought to the sacred lodge in a robe supported by four young men who laid her at the foot of the Medicine Pole. The Master came forward and announced to the people, "I am honored by our Chief to treat his daughter in my humble way. The pledge by our Chief and his household to support the lodge every year will make the heart of the Thunder Bird glad. It is he who will treat the young woman who has come here to attend the dance." Then he instructed the Singers to start a certain song to which every dancer in the lodge danced while the spectators stood quietly in their places. The Master danced for a time near the Medicine Pole. After several verses had been sung he stepped to the east side of the pole. In his left hand he held a hollow buffalo horn with the outside painted a vermillion color. He extended the horn to the audience, turning it upside down to show it was empty. Then he held it to the pole with the edge placed in one of the zigzag grooves. He tapped the pole far above the horn with the tip of the eagle wing fan which he held in his right hand.

At that stage of the ceremony, while the song continued, the small drums, which accompanied the large hide drum, were raised high above the heads of the Singers and beaten with quick, sharp, rhythmic blows. All eyes, full of confidence, were on the master Medicine Man. Some prayed silently for the performer, others that the Thunder Bird would send the medicine water that was sorely needed for the sick young woman.

As the headman tapped gently along the grooved lines water trickled down from it into the horn until it was brim full. Then there were sighs of relief for the people had prayed that this might happen.

The song continued to the end. After it was finished the Medicine Man allowed the young woman to drink as much of the water as she wished. That which remained in the container was sprinkled about the lodge and among the spectators.

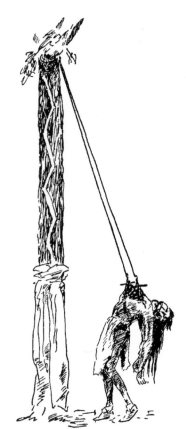

MEDICINE LODGE POLE

PART VI

MEDICINE MEN AND SPIRITS

Men with Magic

Death and the Spirit Bundle

The Spirit World

Journey of the Spirit

Men With Magic

THE TERM MEDICINE MAN, when applied to Indian custom, meant a person who possessed divine power. He treated the sick, forecast events, conducted religious ceremonies, and took part in many gatherings of a religious nature.

The people had confidence in the acts of the medicine man because they knew that if he performed a false rite he or a member of his family would meet with some kind of misfortune. Therefore he could do no wrong.

The medicine men and women were taught by supernatural Beings who appeared to them in dreams or visions. These visits by the Beings were prompted by a prolonged fast and by the many sacrifices made to them.

There were many ways of practicing these powers granted by the Beings; so each man and woman conducted ceremonies differently and according to the way they had been instructed. The use of different objects and the rules governing the people who attended the gatherings had to be followed strictly.

Some old medicine men and women had been given the right to teach younger persons. Often it was a child who had been cured of a very serious illness by the medicine man or woman. In order to cure the child he had imparted his power to it, and that was the reason the child must carry on when it was old enough.

These children were always brought to religious events and taught to take part. The parents saw to it that they sat beside their benefactors and instructors. They also wore sacred bags made by the healers.

To call a medicine man or woman, relatives of a sick person took him a medicine pipe filled with tobacco and other gifts. If the illness was grave they brought one or more horses to the lodge of a medicine man. The visitors placed their hands on his head and beseeched him to accept the fee and treat their sick one. If he accepted, he lit the pipe and smoked it and the goods were left in his lodge or the horses were tied outside.

A call was always paid for in advance. The people understood the rule: "Goods and horses that make up the fees are sacrifices made to the Beings who give the medicine men and women the power to heal." So no one murmured, and the fees were left with the medicine man for the Being who must be pleased.

The medicine man made the call and with the help of one or more singers administered to the sick. He also prayed aloud and mentioned that he was honored to be the agent of the Being whom he named. After a time he converted the fees to his own use. "The Being was through with them," he said.

Medicine men did not name their fees, but either hinted or had someone else suggest them. Sometimes, it is told, a wicked one, who coveted certain objects or the horses of another and had the power to charm, caused a member of the family owning those things to become afflicted with some form of illness.

After others had been called in and had failed to make a cure, he passed word around in such a way that it would reach the family that if he were called he could cure the sick person. After he was called and had attended the sick one, he caused the affliction to remain if the coveted object was not presented. But when the desired fee was given he lifted the charm and the patient recovered. So he not only received what he wanted, but he was praised because of his cure.

There were good medicine men, too, who by means of their power saw the works of the wicked ones and told

MEDICINE CHARM

of the kind of spell which was cast; but for some reason they never revealed the identity of the charmer. They always said: "I could not get a glimpse of his face to know who he is. He always covers his face with his blanket and turns his back to me."

If a sick person died and a charmer was suspected, sometimes relatives of the deceased plotted and killed the medicine man.

Besides the medicine men, there were also herb doctors in each tribe who treated the sick with herbs. Many old women dealt in that kind of thing.

Some medicine men and women also used herbs with their magic treatments. After the religious performance, they gave the patient herbs with directions for their use. Usually these directions were rigid and had to be followed to the letter if a cure was to be effective.

Treatments with herbs were restricted to certain rules laid down by the doctor, which had to be followed. A fee was paid, the same as to a medicine man. Anyone could collect different kinds of herbs for their own use. If persons wanted to know the kind of plants from which certain herbs were obtained, they paid a large fee to an herb doctor who showed them the plants.

The herb doctors got their knowledge of the different kinds of plants for medicinal use in visions, and the informer (a Being) was promised the fees received. After the herbs were dug, offerings were deposited in the hole and carefully covered with dirt.

YOUNG MEN WHO COVETED CERTAIN MAIDENS, paid large fees to herb doctors to charm the girls so that they would return their affection. The love medicine was administered either with or without a ceremony. There were many kinds of charms. Some were made of a mixture of herbs and objects placed in a small ornamented bag, which was carried on the person only during courting time. If the rules were not followed to the letter, the charm would not work.

Some paid a fee to a charmer who performed a ceremony. A form of a male and another of a female were cut out of birchbark and marked as the man and woman. The charmer mentioned the name of each party and then tied the two pieces together face to face in the form of a dummy package. If the young man was fortunate and obtained a lock of the maiden's hair (sometimes the lover paid someone to steal a lock of hair for him), this was wrapped around to bind the two together. The dummy was usually hidden in the woods. After the charm worked, if the maiden was dissatisfied with the man, she went to another charmer who released her for a fee.

Sometimes a woman, who was bought or given in marriage to an older man whom she did not love, left her husband and went to the lodge of her parents. If she refused to come back, the husband paid a charmer who sang and beat on a small high drum for several evenings. He predicted that the woman would return of her own accord before the fourth day. No herbs were used; only the fee was offered as a sacrifice.

THE NORTHERN BANDS WERE NOTED for their possession of a medicine which increased speed and gave stamina to the runners. The medicine was made from herbs, but the mixture and directions for its use was known only to certain medicine men. Runners gave useful things to those men and obtained the medicine for use on special occasions. The northern Assiniboine runners were always accused of using medicine if they won at a gathering where two or more bands entered their best runners. But they were not disqualified as no one had proof that medicine was used.

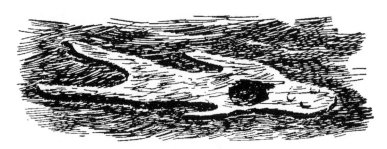

A MEDICINE SYMBOL

They carried a small ornamented bag, which contained the mixture, attached to the belt at the hips. But other kinds of medicine were also carried in the same way, so the bags did not always contain the kind the runners had used. Just before a race, the owner secretly chewed some of the herbs, and unobserved, he smeared a little of the juice on his feet. When the race started he ran just behind the other runners and in their tracks, so the medicine would charm them. When near the goal the runners speeded up and won.

Some suspicious runners always kept far to either side in case some one in the group used a charm, for it is told that the medicine worked only when the keeper ran over the tracks of the others.

CHARMS USED FOR FAST HORSES WERE MADE from parts of fast animals and swift flying birds—such as the tips of the tails of foxes, the short prongs from the horns of antelopes and, for long-winded horses, the ends of wolf tails. The tailfeathers from swift hawks or falcons were the most popular among the charms made from birds.

These animal charms were attached to plain buckskin strings or to ornamented narrow bands. They were hung around the necks of horses, far down, so that the charm lay between the points of the shoulders. Bird feather charms were always tied somewhere on the tails of horses.

There was no secret about the charms used for horses. Even in a gathering, where the horses ran for wagers, the charms were openly attached to the horses. But to win over a horse wearing a charm was also an achievement known to have happened at times.

Men who were skilled in magic were often paid to locate lost horses and other objects for their owners.

THIS STORY ABOUT MAGIC WAS TOLD BY SHOOTS THEM, of the Rock Band: "I am a half blood, my father was white (Alverz, a Spaniard) and my mother was an Assiniboine.

BEAR CLAW CHARM

"Johnson Ryder and I were born the same night and we grew up together among the whites at Fort Union. We learned the Assiniboine language from our mothers and English from our fathers. So, naturally, we did not believe in all that the medicine men said or did.

"After we moved to Wolf Point, Montana, we both were employed in the Indian Agency's blacksmith shop. We were still unmarried.

"For several weeks Johnson's mother was very sick. As there was no white doctor near, in desperation they finally called in a medicine man named Cuwicoga or Center of the Body, who was considered a noted healer and charmer. He was much feared because he made magic many times openly before different crowds.

"He instructed that a large rock be brought and a lodge erected over it in which he would perform his magic.

"We wanted to find out if the sick woman would react to his treatment and said, 'I am going to ask my helper (Being) if this woman is going to get well.'

"He did not attempt to treat Johnson's mother, but first made magic in the lodge.

"So we plotted together to test the power of the man. We hitched a team to a stone boat and brought a rock that probably weighed six hundred pounds.

"We sat together inside the lodge near the entrance and watched every move. There were several singers who also played on drums.

"It was now dusk. The man stripped to just a clout. His body was painted all over with vermillion-colored paint. He instructed his men to tie him with long rawhide thongs. They laced his fingers and toes together with smaller thongs and fastened his hands behind him by tying the two thumbs together.

"They next wrapped a blanket around him and wound the larger thongs over the blanket from head to foot. A half hitch was made each round at the back, so when they were finished, there was a row of half hitches from the back of his neck to his feet.

"A stout thong was tied across the lodge and he hopped over to it and gently sat down on the thong as in a swing.

"The singers started up and the fire was allowed to die down, so we were in semidarkness.

"What followed never was clear to either of us. The man kept saying, 'Do not stop the singing, he is trying to take me with him,' meaning his Spirit Helper.

"When the large rock moved about in that charmed lodge we were scared out of our wits and huddled together in fear. Johnson claimed I crowded him, while I said the same thing of him.

"The rock actually hit the floor of the lodge twice in succession as though it had been raised up and allowed to drop.

"The medicine man shrieked in a distressed voice and said to light up the fire at once. The fire was quickly lit and, when our eyes became accustomed to the light, we saw him high up in the lodge and tucked behind the poles.

"The singers hurried over and helped him down. The thongs had already been removed and coiled together into neat piles, each size in a separate pile on the floor of the lodge with the blanket alongside. He came near the fire and complained of the rough treatment accorded him by the Being. Then he spoke to us and to those who sat outside. He said that the sick woman was even now on the way to complete recovery.

"Johnson's mother lived many years after that. The rock that scared us so badly is still at the old ruins, where he used to live, east of Wolf Point."

Death and the Spirit Bundle

UPON THE DEATH OF AN ASSINIBOINE, A MESSENGER was sent to call a prominent warrior who was a friend of the family. The man entered the lodge, first telling of a war deed; then he cut a liberal amount of hair from the temple of the deceased which he took home with him.

The body was dressed in fine clothing, or the ceremonial dress owned by the deceased; then it was placed in a tanned robe. The whole was next wrapped with an untanned hide, secured with thongs. The body was laid on the branches of a tree, where several crosspieces were tied to the limbs and then tied fast with thongs.

Bodies of warriors and chiefs, if they had wished it, were sometimes burned in their lodges. Some were dressed and laid in the back part of the lodges, while others were placed in sitting positions against back rests and facing the entrance.

When a lodge burial was made, all of the weapons, ceremonial regalia, sacred bundle and other personal property was placed in the lodge in the regular way as though the owner was living. The flap was closed and from the outside long pieces of wood were placed against it. Large rocks were laid around the bottom of the lodge. All this was done to keep animals from entering the lodge. After a lodge burial the people moved to another place.

Personal effects were buried with the body at the request of relatives or if the deceased had wished it. Otherwise, they were given away.

Belongings of children and youths were always given to their playmates, except a boy's horse, whose mane was clipped and tail cut short as an act of mourning for its owner. The horse was not ridden again until the father or brother rode it in the parade at a celebration. Afterwards, many gifts were given away. Sometimes, before the mourning was ended, a relative rode the horse and joined a war party.

Medicine bags, sacred bundles and the large sacks containing the herbs of medicine men and women or herb doctors were always buried with them, unless the man or woman had trained a son or daughter to carry on. Even then, a lot of old medicine things were placed in the burial place. The rattle used by the medicine man or woman was always buried with the body.

CLOSE RELATIVES OF THE DEAD CUT THEIR HAIR SHORT and gashed their arms and legs. Sometimes another person did it for them. Then they dressed in very old clothing and retired to the outer edge of the encampment and lived in seclusion in old six-hide lodges, which were the smallest size made. Distant relatives and friends loosened their hair and wore it for a time upbraided. All of these things were done as acts of mourning.

The man who took the lock of hair also gathered goods and sometimes horses, if the deceased was from a well-to-do family. The relatives did the same, but not jointly with the man. The goods were kept separately.

About a year later, a double lodge was erected and both collections placed there in two piles. The people were all invited to attend. The mourners, dressed in new clothing, their hair braided and faces painted by the sponsors of the feast, were seated inside. Then the man came, bearing an ornamented bundle which contained the lock of hair. He told of a war deed and then placed the bundle in the arms of the father, or the nearest relative, of the dead. At that stage, the mourners wept.

The master of the ceremony, who was someone other than the man with the lock of hair, stepped away from the crowd a short distance and called aloud the name of the dead person. (The names of the dead were never spoken out loud except at that ceremony). He invited the spirit of the deceased to attend the feast prepared in its honor. If the burial place was nearby, the man also went to it with the invitation. The period of mourning was then over.

The collections made by the mourners and the man were exchanged. The mourners received the goods and the large new lodge, while the man became the possessor of the opposite collection.

Then the crowd feasted on the food which had been prepared and the ceremony ended.

THE LOCK OF HAIR OF A DECEASED PERSON WAS ALWAYS KEPT in a bundle hung on a tripod and placed in the back of the lodge. A wide ornamented piece of hide was attached to the middle of the bundle and sometimes the piece was wrapped completely around it. If the lodge was to be used for a gathering, the tripod was placed outside, close behind the lodge. When the band traveled, the bundle was tied to a travois or women packed it, just as they did small children, on their backs.

The spirit bundle was respected, because it was believed to represent the deceased persons. No unnecessary noise was permitted while it was inside the lodge. Children were told not to play near it and not touch it.

All new possessions were first offered to the bundle and left on or near it for several days before being used by the family. Food was offered to it, as a grace, before each meal.

If the deceased was a young man, the father and mother were particularly mindful of the bundle that contained their son's hair. Indian families were never large and he may have been an only son, so the father and mother, as they advanced in years, delighted in things done in remembrance of him.

Sometimes the mother prepared food and invited several young men who had been his friends. The old folks called them their sons because they now took the place of the departed one. Perhaps there was one among them who had lost his mother and he, too, found comfort in the new relationship.

There were evenings when the mother prepared a dish that had been her son's favorite and the old couple partook of it together, alone. But they did not feel that they were alone because, before the meal, the father raised the dish towards the bundle and invited the spirit saying, "Come, my son, your mother has prepared this for you. It is a dish you were always fond of."

In the hallowed presence of the spirit of the youth, the mother was silent, but the father carried on a conversation filled with emotion. He found much comfort, as he told of things and events that had happened, speaking as though the young man had only been away and just returned.

THE DEATH WATCH

The Spirit World

THE ASSINIBOINE BELIEVED THAT SPIRITS of the dead journeyed towards the east. There were medicine men who claimed they had power to bring them back. So when a sick person was in a coma, a medicine man was called in and a sacrifice made, after which he made medicine.

He painted his whole body with white clay to resemble a ghost and wore only his clout and moccasins. In each hand, he carried a rattle. He sang several songs, then while the drummers kept time, he ran towards the east for some distance. He returned and, if successful, explained that he had headed off the spirit.

If the patient came out of the coma, the spirit was surely brought back.

The grandfather of Pointing Down, himself now an old man, told of his experience in the spirit world. He had smallpox when he was young. Whole families died in their lodges. Other people came and folded up the smoke flaps and barricaded the entrances. That served as their burial.

In the lodge where my grandfather lay ill with the disease two other members of the family were dead and their bodies were left where they died. Many families fled to other parts of the country.

Grandfather was so near death that the surroundings did not matter a great deal. He said, "I was very ill, but I noticed that a person looked in, and perhaps thought the three of us were dead. He secured the doorway, piled objects against it, and closed up the smoke hole.

"Sometime after that, I seemed to fall asleep and the next thing I knew, I was outside, walking toward where the sun rises. I traveled along a narrow path that seemed to be on an upgrade. After going in that direction for some time, I came to where a man sat with his back to me. When he turned around, I recognized him as a person who had died some time before.

"The man said: 'Perhaps you want to know where your folks live. I will tell you. There is a large encampment over that hill and the lodge painted blue belongs to your parents.' When I entered the lodge, I saw my father and mother there. My father was busy with some wood he was shaving. My mother, too, was busy at some task.

"With a smile, I said to them: I had no trouble to find your lodge. My mother did not seem to hear me, but my father looked up and stared at me without any sign that he recognized me. I became uneasy, and hesitated to

"With a smile I said to them: 'I had no trouble to find your lodge.'"

take my usual place in their lodge. After a time I went out and looked around for someone to whom I could talk. I recognized several persons and attempted to talk to them, but each time I was not answered.

"I finally retraced my steps and knew I was on the right path, because I came back to the place where the man sat. He spoke: 'You did not stay long, my friend, perhaps someone has come to take you back.' I do not remember if I made any answer.

"I hurried back along the trail and arrived at our lodge. The entrance was barred and I said to myself: How can I go in through the smoke hole, the poles are too close together there. Then a voice awakened me, it was my sister's. She said: 'My brother, you are alive, your eyes are open.' She told me how they decided to flee to some other part, as did the others, and she had said to them: 'For the last time I want to see the body of my brother.'

"That was how she found me and through her help I recovered."

OUTSIDE THE DEATH LODGE

Journey of the Spirit

DUCK WAS AN OLD MAN, PAST SEVENTY, who belonged to the Paddler Band of the Assiniboine tribe which roamed on both sides of the Missouri River west of the mouth of the Yellowstone River. He told this story:

My father, Hatch, which means A Young Thunder Bird Just Hatched, was one of three chiefs of this band. One time when he was a young single man he was in a war party of twelve braves that stole some horses during the night from a camp of the Piegans.

"The Piegans discovered their loss at daybreak. A large group of their warriors started after the horses and overtook the Assiniboines, who had taken refuge in a heavily wooded ravine near the north side of the Missouri River.

"A hot battle took place with an overwhelming number of Piegans surrounding the Assiniboines. The Piegans rode round and round shooting into the ravine, and killing all the stolen horses except one. But none of the men were hit.

"A FIERCE BATTLE TOOK PLACE WITH AN OVERWHELMING NUMBER OF
PIEGANS SURROUNDING THE ASSINIBOINES."

"Late in the afternoon of the second day, the fighting subsided somewhat and occasionally a small group would charge near the edge of the brush and shoot into it, then retreat to the main line.

"It was on one of those skirmishes when the Piegans were retreating to their line, that one of their number remained behind still shooting. My father, being young and wishing to make a name for himself, jumped out of the timber and ran straight for this man. It happened so suddenly that the act took both parties by surprise. The man shot once and turned and ran, but my father overtook him and felled him with a war hatchet. Then he fell on top of the Piegan and, being winded, lay there for a brief moment. Then he heard a slight noise above. He looked up quickly and saw a Piegan pointing a gun at him. The next instant there was a report. All this happened like the flip of a beaver's tail.

"My father was shot through the head, the bullet entering just below the right cheek bone, passed through the mouth and came out below the ear.

"The Piegans did not stop to scalp my father but jerked off the hatchet that he used which hung from a loop around his wrist, in such a rush that his wrist was lacerated. Then they fled back to their line with the body of their dead.

"When the Assiniboines realized that one of their number was lying dead between the skirmish lines, they all charged the enemy and brought back the body of my father to the ravine.

"It was a great war act on the part of both the Piegans and Assiniboines to be able to recover their fallen ones before they were scalped or counted coup.

"That night the Assiniboines decided to leave, as they had not eaten a good meal for two days. My father's body was slung on the only horse left alive and, leading it, they quietly slipped out following the ravine to the Missouri River. By daybreak they were out of danger of any further attack. They erected a lodge of poles with the branches left on and covered it with willows for protection again animals. There they placed my father's body in a sitting position.

"After a day's journey homeward, my father's brother, Beaver Cap, was reluctant to go any farther. He said, 'My brother is dead but his body is still warm. I am going back to look once more to make sure that he is dead.'

"So the rest of them said, 'We will wait for you here till you return.'

"When Beaver Cap reached the burial lodge he pushed the branches aside and peeped in and spoke, saying, 'My brother, I have come back once more to make sure that you have really gone east to join our departed relatives.'

"As he spoke the eye lids of the dead man moved ever so slightly but enough to arrest the attention of Beaver Cap. He tore the branches apart and rushed into the lodge. He felt of the heart beat and was satisfied that his brother was alive. He spoke again and again but there was no response.

"Beaver Cap hurriedly retraced his steps back to the waiting party and told them what he had seen. They all went back to the lodge and made preparations to move my father.

"They cut down two cottonwood trees and made a travois, leaving the leaves and branches intact to make riding easier for him. In this manner my father was brought back to his people. He become conscious but it was many days before he could talk, as the wound in his mouth had paralyzed his tongue.

"He later told me the sensation of being shot and of being dead. He heard the report of the gun and that was all. When he thought he had regained consciousness, he felt that he was moving rapidly through the air. As he traveled along, he realized that he did not have his black stone medicine pipe, which he never failed to carry with him. Not being in possession of it caused him no little worry. He slackened his pace and finally stopped, saying to himself, 'I must go back after my pipe before I go any farther.' He turned about and the next thing he heard was voices. Rousing himself as out of a deep sleep, he tried to say something but could not make a sound. Then he heard his father say, 'My son, look at me, I am your father.'

"My father lived many years afterwards but the wound always bothered him. One day he told my brothers and me that he would soon die. It was only a short time after this that, as my mother was preparing the noon meal, my father reached down to take the food and fell over and died very suddenly."

PART VII

COMING OF THE WHITE MEN

The Ones Who Paddle a Canoe

Lone White Man

Meeting With The Sioux

Treaties and Reservation Life

The Ones Who Paddle a Canoe

MANY, MANY WINTERS AGO, when our people traveled on foot and used dog travois to carry their belongings, and the weapons consisted of bows, arrows and stone clubs, it was told that a medicine man had a vision, in which a Being appeared.

This legend was recounted by Dry Bone, from Sintaluta, Saskatchewan, Canada as told to him by Braids in Middle of the Fort Belknap Reservation:

The Supreme One said to him, "Select four strong young warriors among your people, for you will lead them on a journey across the big water that extends away from your land. When you have gathered your young men together, make sacrifices and I will tell you more about my plan."

The medicine man invited many likely warriors to his lodge and told them of his vision.

"Talk it over among yourselves," He told them, "I will leave the selection to you men. Whoever the four may be, they will make a name for themselves."

It was no easy task to form a crew of that kind. Many excuses were made by parents, relatives and sweethearts; for this was a journey so different from a war party. A journey across so large a body of water where no man ever

had gone before did not appeal to them. But finally there appeared four braves who said they were the chosen four.

The journey was not started at once, but preparations for it were made with much excitement. The tribe considered the adventure a dangerous one, for it was believed that the party would never return.

The leader finally received instructions from the Being, to the effect that round hide-boats should be made for each man and that each boat should be loaded with two kinds of pemmican. One kind was to consist of pounded chokecherries and pounded dried buffalo meat mixed with buffalo marrow fat. The other was to be of pounded dried buffalo meat with chunks of hard tallow. Good bows and many arrows, together with the necessary clothing, were to be part of the equipment. The final instruction was for the medicine man to make eagle feathers, dyed in many colors, into a large bundle.

When all preparations were completed, the medicine man and the four braves paddled away with farewells from their people on the shore. Some of the people sang the death song while others sang songs of encouragement and praise.

This water was dotted with many islands and no one could see to the other shore. The trip across that vast sea took many days. Each evening the party tied up at one of the islands for the night. Occasionally, when the sign of a storm approached, the leader took one of the colored feathers and dropped it into the water as an offering. Later, when a sea monster appeared near them, a feather offering was immediately made to it. In that way the journey proceeded smoothly. At the islands, feathered and small game were taken with their bows and arrows.

After many days, a long black cloud was noted on the horizon and on approaching closer it turned out to be land. When the party arrived ashore, they saw other human beings; but their faces were covered with hair like their heads.

The Assiniboines were afraid of them, but by signs and gestures conversation was carried on. The party was given food and told to rest from their journey.

The travelers had come to the land of the white race, it was explained to them.

During the night the medicine man had a visit from the Being, who said, "You have arrived at the end of your journey. These people that you see will not harm you but they will help you and your people to live better. It is because their weapons are much better than your bows and arrows. Such will be given to you and you will be taught how to use them. Other things to use and to wear will also be made known to you."

Next day the white men called the Indians together and showed them a gun. They were taught how to load and to fire it. At first the report frightened them and the recoil knocked them down, but finally they were able to master it and use it as their teachers did. That took many days; and many more days were needed to learn other things that were used by the white people.

A large boat with many sails was loaded with guns, ammunitions, food, clothing, utensils, tools, and trinkets. When all was ready the Indians were told to go on board and direct the way to their land.

After many days, the boat arrived at the shore from which the party had started, but no one was in sight. The people had fled into the woods at the sight of the large boat, it was believed.

The medicine man and his four young men went ashore and called to their people. No one appeared for a long time. Then finally a spokesman came forward and looked them over. When he was satisfied that they were the party that had left on a journey many moons ago, he said, "Speak up, my friends, tell me that you are alive and that it is not your spirits who have returned. Explain the meaning of the large boat with wings. Has the Being brought you back?"

"It is I and my four young men," said the medicine man. "We have brought our people good words; we have brought friends who will teach us many new things. Go back, call our people together in council so our friends will meet them."

So a crier was sent who called the people together. A council was held that welcomed the brave travelers and the white men they had brought with them.

And so, that was the way the Assiniboine, known as 'The Ones Who Paddle a Canoe,' met the whites for the first time.

Lone White Man

LONG BEFORE THE TRIBE MET THE WHITES, many of the white man's weapons, tools, utensils and goods were introduced to them through French half-breeds. Most of these half-breeds spoke the Assiniboine language and acted as agents for white traders who were employees of the Hudson's Bay Company.

One of the many stories told about this, is related by the old man Last:

"My father told that the French breeds came in winter with sleds drawn by dogs. They were dressed in wolf skins, had much goods and white fire-water. This they mixed with water and gave away while the trade was in progress. The tribe traded furs, tanned robes and dried meat with them.

"I have seen them too, when I was a young man, and their methods of trading were no different from the first time as my father described it.

"Another story, told by Mrs. Crazy Bull, who is ninety, is:

"The Paddlers, a Missouri River band that occupied the country east of the mouth of the Yellowstone River, were said to be the first who met the whites. The white men were, 'The Ones That Pulled the Boat.'"

Another told by Nick Alverz:

"My father, Philip Alverz, was a member of an expedition that came up the Missouri River. (Both informants believed this to be the Lewis and Clark expedition). He told that they first saw the Assiniboine near the mouth of the White Earth River.

"My father left the party on the return trip down the river and stayed with the Rock Band of the tribe where he married my mother. The expedition was known as, 'Travelers Pulling a Boat,' or more correctly in our language, *Watgaska Ayabi,* meaning 'pulled a boat on a journey' ".

STILL ANOTHER MAN, BAD HAWK, TELLS THIS STORY:

"My granduncle, Tall Man, was a member of a war party of about twelve, that camped on the south side of the Missouri River, above where the Government has built the great Fort Peck Dam.

"When the party resumed their journey early the next morning, the two scouts, who had left earlier, came running back. 'There is a strange man walking towards the river with a gun on his shoulder,' they said. So the party circled about and hid in the path of the man.

"When he came closer, one from the party rose and walked towards him, at the same time lifting his hand as a sign for the man to stop. In sign language he was asked as to what tribe he belonged, but instead of an answer the man dropped his gun and raised his hands high above his head.

"The rest of the party, when they saw the act, ran over and surrounded the man. Several spoke up, 'Don't any of you kill him, he is a different kind of man, let's look him over.'

"He stood there terrified and continued to look from one to the other.

"The man was tall and his hair was down to his shoulders. With the exception of his forehead, eyes and nose, his face was covered with a heavy beard. His chest, his arms down to the tops of his hands, and his legs were covered with a hairy growth. Nothing like that had ever been seen among the tribe, only animals were that way.

" 'This must be what is called a white man, that we have heard about,' they said among themselves.

"His clothing was torn to shreds and he was thin and seemed to be starved. Apparently all he had had for food were several pieces of a large cactus that he had peeled. These he kept in the shot bag that was attached to the powder horn. They took him along, made camp right away and prepared some food which he devoured like a hungry animal.

"He stayed with the war party until they returned home. Fortunately for the white man there were no encounters with the enemy on that trip.

"My granduncle took the man home and new clothing was made for him. The man gave the gun, which was without ammunition, to my granduncle. He stayed with our people for many years and my granduncle adopted him as a brother, because they were about the same age and height. He was named Lone White Man."

"When he learned our language, he told of being with a party of white men that came up the Missouri River. He was with a group of hunters who supplied game for the party. When the crew started their journey up stream each day, the hunters traveled away from the river, then parallel with it until they joined the crew at the night camp with game killed that day.

"On one of those jaunts, Lone White Man failed to meet the party. Each day he expected to find them but after several days he came to the conclusion that he was lost. As he had enough ammunition to last only a day or so, it was not long before he was out entirely. Berries and roots were all he had to eat after that.

"On the morning that he was seen by the war party, he was on his way to the river, thinking he might see a boat. He had kept near the river all the time hoping to find his party.

"Even after the whites were numerous, Lone White Man showed no desire to leave our people. One day he met one of the steamboats and did some trading. Among other things, he brought home some bacon and a frying pan. He told my granduncle that he had wanted fried liver and bacon for so long that he was going to satisfy that desire. He prepared a large stack of fried liver and bacon on which he feasted all alone. With so many different kinds of meat to be had at that time, our people never ate liver, which they used only for tanning hides.

"Lone White Man lived among our people for many years, but never married. Granduncle never told if the man died out here or finally left the country."

Meeting with the Sioux

THE STORY OF HOW THE ASSINIBOINE PEOPLE AND THE SIOUX, who now live together as friends, first met on this basis, is told by Red Feather:

"The Sioux were known to our people many years ago. But they were our enemies. The first friendly contact was made, I was told, at the big bend of the Mouse River, before my time. One of our hands was camped there and four Sioux, all young men, came on a friendly mission.

"The purpose of their visit could not have been very important, because very little was said about it. The meeting was not mentioned as an event, merely as the first time members of the Sioux visited our people in a friendly way.

"The first time that a band of the Sioux came among our people, was when I was about thirteen years old. That meeting is considered an event to this day, as you will see.

"We were camped east of the mouth of the White Earth River and it was midsummer. My father and I had been away, on horseback, and when we

"IN ORDER TO FEED THE REFUGEE BAND OF SIOUX, MANY DOGS WERE KILLED AND COOKED. NOTHING WAS WASTED."

came within view of our camp, we saw a caravan near our circle. We watched for a few moments and my father said that the people did not look like any of our bands. When we got there we were told that the people were the Santee band of the Sioux. They were camped beside our camp. They looked tired and worn out from their long journey.

"These people were in a starved condition. They told that they had fled from a massacre in what is now Minnesota and had come across a country where there was almost no game. Their only food had been wild turnips, berries, and such small game as they could find. The women had long iron bars with which they dug turnips.

"One of our camp criers came by and said, 'Our headmen have asked you to gather food and to feed our visitors, for they are starving.' "In summer there was never much food in a camp. Every few days the people were on the move to new locations where game was plentiful. In order to feed the refugee band, many dogs were killed and cooked up. Nothing of the dogs was wasted, even the intestines and stomachs were cleaned, cooked, and eaten by these poor people.

"The crier came around again the next day and proclaimed that all hunters were asked to procure meat for all of the people, because the two bands being together had upset the regular food supply of the camp.

"Several Sioux children were given away among our people in exchange for food. Two of them lived among our people until they died. One of them was a girl named Santee Woman who died near Frazer, Montana about two years ago. The other one, a lad, went by the name of Santee. He later married into a northern band of our tribe and died not many years ago in Canada. Both of them were named after their band name, Santee."

SIOUX FROM MINNESOTA MASSACRE.

Treaties and Reservation Life

AFTER THE WHITE MEN CAME THE FIRST SO-CALLED "TREATIES" were made between agents of the early fur companies and different bands of the Assiniboine tribe. An agreement made by a band was not binding on other bands. It was a pact only between that band and the Factor, covering hunting and trading, boundaries, delivery of furs and other items of this nature.

Usually in concluding such a pact the agent of a fur company invited the Chief of a band to the trading post. There the Chief was clothed in some showy uniform, usually of a military design. Agents of the Hudson's Bay Company, for example, almost always gave British uniforms. They often presented the Chief with a sword. His wife and children, too, were usually given presents.

In return the Chief promised to turn the trade of his people to that Post.

THE FIRST AND MOST IMPORTANT TREATY between the Assiniboine Nation and the United States Government was the Treaty of Fort Laramie, consummated on

September 17, 1851, in Indian Territory. The tribe was represented at this great meeting by First Fly and Crazy Bear, chiefs of their bands.

Although not all of the bands were represented, the whole tribe later recognized this treaty as binding on all Assiniboine bands in the United States.

A copy of the treaty and the silver medal received by First Fly was buried with his body at death and lost forever to the tribe. But the stipulations of the original treaty, printed on sheepskin, and a silver medal, were handed down from Crazy Bear to the present leader, Many Voices, known to the whites as Joseph Matthew, sixth Chief of the Assiniboine, who is the official custodian.

After the Treaty of Fort Laramie, the tribe settled on the old Milk River Reservation and a start was made in accepting the new mode of living.

The Indian Bureau set up a head agency and several subagencies on the reservation with a white agent and a staff of employees (subagents, clerks, Indian police and laborers) conducting affairs. All rules and regulations were sent out from the Indian Office at Washington, D. C., to be carried out by the local agent and his staff.

In the earliest reservation days the Indians who had ruled themselves well for centuries found they no longer had a voice in their government. They had to obey the government rules or go to jail. An Indian judge who was also the prosecuting attorney was appointed to uphold the white man's laws. His salary was $8.00 a month, and there were two court days in each month.

When persons were sentenced by this judge, they were sent to what was known as the guardhouse, or jail. Prisoners received sentences ranging from ten to ninety days. If the offense was of a serious nature, they were sometimes shackled and confined in a room with barred windows. There was no such thing as a parole.

Other prisoners did chores about the agency grounds under a guard. Many of them wore the ball and chain, while some were hobbled with a chain hobble. Both practices later were discontinued.

THE PEOPLE IN THOSE DAYS RECEIVED RATIONS TWICE A MONTH. Every second week several beef cattle were butchered and on the following day the people were issued such items as fresh meat, salted bacon, flour, sugar and coffee.

Land was then owned in common so when a person died there was no estate left. All possessions were left to the relatives to do with as they saw fit.

The white buffalo hunters, who unmercifully slaughtered the animals for their hides, had almost exterminated the buffalo by the time the Assiniboine were placed on the reservation. When the buffalo perished, a few years later, the main meat supply was gone. During the winter of 1883 and 1884, due to poor transportation, annuities were not received and more than three hundred persons died of starvation at the Wolf Point Subagency Station, where the tribe then wintered.

The Indian Bureau gradually changed its rules and regulations with the times. Today many of the unfortunate things that happened under earlier supervision seem unbelievable, yet there is still much room for improvement.

AFTER 1884 THE TRIBE COMMENCED to scatter along the southern boundary of the reservation in the Missouri River valley. Not all at once, but gradually, families moved away from the Indian town around the agency. At first a chief or headman started a village with his band around him; finally there were six such villages established along the Missouri River bottom.

Ration day was every other Wednesday and the preceding Sunday found the tribe camped as of old in a circle near the agency. The bands from different villages were grouped side by side in the camp circle. Usually a circular dance hall was built in the center of such a camp site. The building was of logs and had a dirt roof. Here dances were held until after ration day. By Friday the bands had dispersed and returned to their villages.

Now and then, in season, groups camped out after game, gathered turnips or picked berries. They returned to the agency campgrounds before the next ration day.

These villages existed until the old heads of families died and their children married and went to other parts of the reservation.

The land was owned in common but each family marked an area that it claimed. There were no disputes and no fences were set up to enclose the land except the garden tracts.

The people lived in a leisurely way through that period. They were rationed, clothed, given tools, machinery, stock, medical attention and education for their children at boarding schools. They lived from one ration period to another until the allotment system went into effect. This created another change in reservation life.

UNDER A TREATY WITH THE GOVERNMENT IN 1908, the tribe agreed to the opening of the Fort Peck Reservation for homesteading by the whites. Engineers were sent to survey and plat an area forty miles wide and eighty miles long. This land was later classified and appraised.

Each Indian enrolled on the reservation, was allotted three hundred and twenty acres of prairie land and forty acres of irrigable land on the Missouri River bottom. Some of those forty-acre tracts were along creeks which the appraisers considered as bottom land. Each head of a family was also allotted twenty acres of timber land.

And so it came about that the Indians who lived wherever they chose in a vast country from time beyond memory, now lived separately, each on their own small piece of land.

In July, 1913, the reservation was opened to the whites, which was the end of the segregation period as far as the tribe was concerned.

After the tribe was given lands, a Mr. Jones came to Wolf Point as sub-agent. He was a farmer and taught the people to plant large gardens. According to old habit it was found that women were the best gardeners.

Because there was much wild hay, breeding stock of horses and cattle were issued to the Assiniboine who took readily to stock raising. In a few years most families had large herds of cattle and horses. Fine horses were raised through use of several breeds of sires that were kept at the agency at stud. Steers were shipped to market every fall by the trainload with the agent and several of the Indian stockmen accompanying the shipments.

But as each succeeding agent came, changes were adopted according to the ideas of the newcomer. Some were good and some were bad. Almost all were confusing to the Indians.

Under one agent, a band of sheep was purchased and a tribal ownership was set up. Later, under another administration, the sheep were sold and young heifers bought and distributed to individuals for foundation stock. Still later, a five-year farming program was started, with part of the tribe's funds set up as a credit revolving fund. The amount was $50,000. The dry years closed that program with the money owed by the Indian farmers.

At the present time an irrigation project is under construction along the Missouri River bottom. This, with improvement of the lands and a reha-bilitation program, looks promising for the tribe, which now has become more accustomed to the white man's way.

THE FIRST GOVERNMENT SCHOOL WAS ESTABLISHED at Poplar, main agency of the Fort Peck Reservation, in 1892. The old military post buildings were used to house the first sixty children.

"Two meals were served each day," a man who attended school there tells. "We got pretty hungry when meal time came around. A lot of boys ran away from the school and went home, but as fast as they got home, the Indian police brought them back. They were punished by whipping and confined in rooms by themselves.

"The two boys who herded the school's milk cows were the best off. They used to suck a black cow that was so obliging that she came over to the herders when her bag was full. Perhaps it relieved her. That went on until the industrial teacher found it out.

"Since the office recorded all births, a check was made each fall and the agent knew who was of school age for the opening term. A list was made and sent to each subagency. The police, in each district, were ordered to bring the children into the Poplar school. The method was strictly compulsory.

"Indian police were hard-boiled in those days. They were uniformed in navy blue suits with brass buttons, wore stiff brim hats with gold cord hat bands that knotted in front. They carried 44-40 calibre revolvers strapped to their hips and each had a carbine of like calibre in a scabbard attached to the saddle. They were mounted, too. The chief wore red stripes on his sleeves and pants legs, down each outer seam. There were at one time thirty on the force but later it was cut down to twenty. Today there are only three for the entire reservation.

"The police delighted in the enforcement of their duties. The first group were men who were warriors and a job which was mingled with danger was welcomed. When the order came to gather the school children, the police went in pairs. One stood outside the lodge entrance and held the horses while the other entered. The police usually took the child by the wrist and marched out with him. There was much weeping and many sad hearts.

"The children were loaded into a wagon, brought along for that purpose, and when a load was gotten together they were taken to the boarding school at Poplar.

"It was no wonder that some of the fathers stood the police off with a gun and there were several times that the entire force was called to arrest a father of a schoolboy or girl who resisted the officers."

Methods changed and the boarding school at Poplar improved with time. New log buildings were added and later several brick structures replaced the old log buildings built by the soldiers. At the peak of attendance in 1898, there were over 300 boys and girls, including Sioux.

It was then a grade school with industrial and domestic training. There were classes all day, but the group that attended the morning classes worked at some trade in the afternoon, and those who worked in the morning went to their classes in the afternoon.

The discipline was along military lines with drill practices for both boys and girls. All wore uniforms and the school had a band and a ball team.

Today the Assiniboine children attend public schools in all of the principal towns on the reservation and a few are enrolled at grade schools in the rural sections. School busses now transport the high school students to larger centers and the reservation is not much different from other places in Montana. The old way of life has almost vanished.

THE END

PART VIII
APPENDICES

The Author

The Illustrator

The Old Ones Who Told The Stories

Assiniboine Bands

Pronunciation Guide

Reading List

PICTURE WRITING
ONLY RECORDED STORIES OF THE LONG AGO DAYS.

The Author

MY NAME IS JAMES LARPENTEUR LONG or First Boy in the Assiniboine. I was born Christmas day, 1888, on the north side of the Missouri River across from Pyramid, an early day steamboat landing, two miles south of what is now Oswego, Montana.

The trading post consisted of a store and a saloon. Nearby was the historic N-N ranch, owned by the Niedringhaus Brothers of St. Louis, Missouri.

My father, James A. Long, was a government official of English descent who came from Hamilton, Ohio to teach the Assiniboine how to farm. My mother, Annie Larpenteur, was the daughter of Charles Larpenteur, a Frenchman who traded with the Indians during Fort Union's heyday. She was born at Fort Union August 15, 1870. Her mother, Makes Cloud Woman, was the only daughter of First Fly, Chief of the Rock People, one of the thirty-three bands that comprised the Assiniboine Nation. First Fly was the son of Wanhi Maza or Iron Arrowpoint, Chief of the Rock Band.

My father died two months before my birth and I was brought up by my mother and grandmother. Being an only child, I was much in company with grown-ups and aged people until I went to the Poplar River Boarding School at the age of seven. After that I always spent my two months vacation in July and August with my mother and grandmother.

In those days there was much game. I did a lot of hunting, first with bow and arrows, later with a muzzle-loader fired by a cap, which, when held upright with the butt on the ground beside me, was taller than I. The gun was brought from Canada by visiting Assiniboine.

At the age of three, I killed a snow bird with a long stick and my grandmother gave a big feast on account of it.

I killed a gray wolf with a 22-calibre pistol after a long chase on horseback when I was thirteen. Although my mother and grandmother never joined in the Circle Dance, yet they got a man to announce my kill at the next dance and many goods were given to the poor in honor of the event.

About two years later, I accompanied my cousin, who was much older than I, on a hunt for coyote pups. Two female coyotes had their litters in a den beneath a large sandstone. I was chosen because of my slenderness to crawl under. An old man named White, a well-known hunter, said, "I have never known a female coyote or wolf to bite a person when they are in a den with their young ones."

With a rope in one hand I crawled in and tied the rope to one of the female's hind legs. I yanked on another rope tied to one of my ankles and the men pulled me out. Then the mother coyote was dragged out and shot. The young ones were pulled out one by one by the use of long willows stripped of all branches with the small ends roughened. These were thrust into the den and turned against the body of a pup. By twisting the roughened end into the fur the animal was caught fast and could be pulled out easily.

The Assiniboine name, First Boy, was given to me at the age of ten by He Wets It, a noted warrior and later in his old age a medicine man. I was proud. The meaning is "a leader among boys."

Several names were also given to me by a survivor of a great battle between forty Assiniboine warriors and about three hundred Sioux, who made the attack on horseback. In this battle, in the northwestern part of now North Dakota, my great grandfather, First Fly, was killed. The Assiniboine were so outnumbered that only a few came back alive, and they were saved by nightfall. Some of the Assiniboine were crowded into a lake and had to swim across to the other side. Many were killed in the water. My war names, Almost Killed, Swims About, and Comes Back Alive, were all taken from this encounter with the Sioux.

At twelve years, I was inducted into the Horse Society, a men's secret organization, on the recommendation of He Wets It who was also my sponsor at the ceremony. When I was about fourteen, the Ghost Dance, a new Indian religion which originated in the south, was introduced among the Assiniboine. I attended a good many of the gatherings. However, my grandmother and mother were Catholics so I was baptized by the Rev. Father Fredrick Hugo Eberschweiler in the midsummer of 1896. Since then I have been active in spreading the white man's religion among our people.

I finished the eighth grade at seventeen and started to work as clerk and chore boy for the Wolf Point Trading Company. The Agency square, where this firm was located, was also an old steamboat landing south of the present town of Wolf Point. We dealt in livestock, hay, wood, hides, wool, pelts, skins, fine furs and many Indian articles. There was little actual money then and business was carried on mostly by barter.

In 1913, I married Mary Knapp, who was one-eighth Assiniboine. She was the daughter of Dan Knapp, an Indian trader at Oswego, who came from Germany as a young man. We had two girls, Phillipena and Anna.

From 1913 to 1919 I raised cattle and horses along the Missouri River bottoms east of Oswego. When my wife died in 1918, I sold my livestock and again became a clerk, this time for my father-in-law, Dan Knapp, in Oswego. When he died in 1923, his nephew, August Knapp, and I bought the business, a general merchandise and hardware stock. We dissolved partnership in the spring of 1938. That fall I started a grocery store in Oswego, where I still live. Here the old Indians gather and tell exploits of days gone by, such as are retold in this book.

In 1920 I married Regina Koch who had come from Missouri with her parents in 1917 to a homestead on the Fort Peck Indian reservation which had been thrown open to white settlers. From this union were born two girls, Maxine and Frances, and a boy, Charles Larpenteur, who died at an early age.

My life has been spent studying my people and working for their interests. I have served four years as a member of the Executive Board of the Tribal Council, a group of twelve which represents the tribe's activities with the Federal Government. I am also one of a committee of five, known as The 1851 Treaty Committee. This committee represents the Assiniboine tribe in its suit against the Government for treaty violations. I am secretary for the resettlement of Indian families on 4,400-acre irrigation unit, a step in the direction of economic use of Indian lands and self-support of the Indian people; and a director of the Fort Peck United Projects to promote power, irrigation and national defense possibilities of the Fort Peck Dam.

Books and papers on the Assiniboine have been written by white men who were traders, scientists, soldiers, missionaries, and others who married into the tribe. In them fact is intermingled with theories. These writers attended a ceremony, for example, and got the meaning of it through an interpreter. Then they added what they thought. Some interpreters are not wholly familiar with a custom or a ceremony; others cannot pass the meaning of it correctly to a researcher. In such cases the writer unintentionally prepares the article in the wrong light. But the fault of most white writers on Indian tribes is the tendency to use their own theories about what they have seen or were told about.

Only a person who is a blood member and has lived in close contact with his people is able thoroughly to understand the true meaning of the customs and ceremonies of the Indian. The meaning and purpose of some of the religious organizations is so deep that words translated into English are meaningless. A person has to be one of them to really understand.

This work by no means tells all about the Assiniboine but it is accurate. Only legends never before published have been used. What has been gathered and written has been done with utmost care through direct information. I talk the language fluently, read and write it as well. I reminded the old people of stories and legends that I had heard when I was a boy. This refreshed their memories and they would then tell the complete story. I am fortunate in knowing the sign language, which is universal among nearly all tribes. Sometimes, in order to interview a deaf person, I had to carry on conversation in this manner.

The Pipe Man from the Spirit Land has already come for the pipes that belonged to several of the Old Ones and they have followed him back to the land of their departed relatives.

The Above Ones were kind to these good-on-earth-people who made the talks that will be passed on to their grandchildren.

The Beings honored them because of their many sacrifices, allowing them to reach the age of deep thinking and gray hairs which made possible whatever merits this book may possess.

JAMES L. LONG

The Illustrator

BECAUSE I AM A FULL-BLOODED ASSINIBOINE, I have different names. In the white men's custom I am William Standing after the first name of my old father, Standing Rattle. My father called me Looks In The Clouds. My own choice of names is Fire Bear; this was my grandfather's name and also the Indian name of my Canadian-Sioux wife.

It makes no difference to me. If people want me to sign a name on pictures in white man's way and buy more that is all right. But I'd rather be Fire Bear.

Some people do not like the way I sometimes draw them and call me other names. That does not bother me much either. Most of us do not look as handsome to others as we do to ourselves. But I like to be what is called an independent artist and draw and paint what I see. Maybe I am something like my ancient ancestor In The Light. He was an independent man too.

PAINTING LODGE DESIGNS—THE OLD TIME ILLUSTRATOR

It is told that long, long ago (1832) In The Light, or Azan-zan-na, was the first one of our Assiniboine people to go to the Great White Father in Washington. He traveled with a Government Indian agent named Major Stanford.

The white men liked to show off all great things he had and In The Light was eager to see everything. He saw the white men's great houses and cities and great forts, ships and bridges. It is told he thought the white council house at Washington was one of the greatest medicine places there could be. He saw big army parades in New York City and a balloon going up in the air, and all other things which even white men thought were great in those long-ago days.

When In The Light returned to our people he is said to have told of strange things he had seen. Our people felt these things could not be true. They called this early ancestor of mine "greatest liar in the world." But he never changed. He told the truth, which they thought was lying. According to Assiniboine customs he became regarded an outstanding medicine man, because he had such strange visions and told such big stories. Some people hated him; some were afraid. Others said he could not be killed by bullets.

Finally In The Light was killed by one of our own people, a man named Mnazana, while he sat in a gathering of men in a lodge. The jealous Mnazana ran to another tribe, the Gros Ventres of the Missouri, to hide. As it was the rule among the Assiniboine for relatives of slain persons to take revenge, Mnazana was trailed and killed in an earth lodge of Gros Ventres.

I have always wanted to draw and paint. Maybe this comes from my mother's side of the family. Her brother Lance was considered a noted painter of medicine lodges.

A story is told that as a small boy I was often unruly. One evening my mother drew the face of an evil spirit on the bottom of a pan and set it in a corner to frighten me so that I would behave. Next morning I found the pan, and erased the ugly face. With wood ashes, I drew a more kindly one. My drawing began at that early age.

The Government agents decided I, like all young Indians, should learn the white men's ways at what they called the agency day school near Oswego. Here I became more like a white man. I took off my leggings and the barbers cut my braids. Then many years later, when I went to Washington to exhibit paintings, the white men decided I looked too much like them and gave me horse hair braids to wear with my Indian clothes.

When I was older they sent me to a boarding school at Wolf Point, known as the Presbyterian Mission. In 1920 I went to the Haskell Institute in Kansas and stayed there four years. I was always painting and drawing but the only training which the teachers gave me in this line was jobs of painting the outside of buildings at the school.

After this school period was over, I was much happier. School kept me too much indoors. I could now go freely and do what I wanted. For a few years I saw a lot of the country in different states. I supported myself by drawing pictures and selling them. Then I came back to the reservation to settle down and be married. I have painted a lot since then.

I am old enough that among my friends are some of the few humpback (buffalo) eaters still alive. Old timers like Walking Bull, Blue Cloud, First Eagle, Shooter and my old father, too, have told me the stories which make me appreciate the old way of life.

I remember when one of my old grandfathers was telling about the hereafter, and came to a point where he hoped he would be hunting the humpbacks again in some country and bringing meat to the lodge. The way he described the Happy Hunting Ground sounded as if we are sure of growing up this time in that country. I think the Happy Hunting Ground ought to be this White Man's Country.

I can understand old time Indian way of life and have tried to show it in the drawings for this book—not the imitation Indian but the real one who hunted humpbacks in good old days.

I asked old timers many questions about the way they cooked meat on a long-ago hunting party, or made a trap for the humpbacks, or dressed up for a grass dance; how bows and arrows looked, medicine pipes or old fashion leggings and moccasins with right designs—not drug store imitations.

When the drawings were finished I showed them to the old timers for approval. There is lot of difference between the way an Indian CCC crew looks at work today and a hundred-year-ago war path party going after Blackfeets or Santees scalps and horses.

Ten summers ago I was in Washington for an exhibit of my paintings at the Washington Art Club. The Vice President, who then was second best to the Great White Father, was Charles Curtis, a part Kaw Indian. The newspapers took pictures of me and the Vice President shaking hands.

This same collection was afterwards sent to a Colonial Art Exhibit in

Paris. My work was also in Colorado, Oklahoma, and other states, in the WPA Art Center at Great Falls and Butte, Montana, and in many other places.

In making the drawings for this book I have tried to help James Long tell young Assiniboines the truth about the old timers. I hope the book will also help the white men understand the Assiniboine's old ways of life.

Maybe my grandfathers and grandmothers in the Happy Hunting Ground will feel better if they know that white men are being more friendly because they understand the old time Red Men better.

WILLIAM STANDING

The Old Ones Who Told the Tales

THE AVERAGE AGE OF THE OLD ONES who told these stories was 77. All the ages listed below were for 1939. More than half of these people are now dead. Many of these people retold stories told them by their grand-and great-grandparents, which in itself dates them back a century and a half to before the Lewis and Clark Expedition. The members of this expedition were the first white men seen by many of the Montana Indian tribes.

Those who told the tales are as follows:

Gabe Beauchman, 105 years, Wolf Point, Montana. Beauchman was born at Fort Union, the son of a white father and an Assiniboine mother. He was a member of the Rock Band. Although he hunted buffaloes which were sold to the Hudson's Bay Company, he had no war record.

Black Dog, 80 years, Wolf Point, Montana. Black Dog, a member of the Prairie Paddler Band, was born near White Earth, North Dakota. He went on several war journeys.

Red Feather, 89 years, Oswego, Montana. Red Feather was born in the northwestern part of what is now North Dakota. He was a famous warrior and participated in thirty-one war trips. At one time he was with a war party that brought back more than thirty horses. He was a member of the Rock Mountain People Band.

Last, 86 years, Oswego, Montana. Last was another famous fighting-man whose name means a warrior who acted as a guard or scout at the rear of a caravan. One time while alone he captured three horses and once counted the fourth coup. He brought back from the enemy line a wounded brother, took two scalps, and on three occasions was in actual war encounter with the enemy. He was born near Berthold, North Dakota and belonged to the Dog Band.

Bad Hawk, 74 years, Oswego, Montana. Bad Hawk was born near Poplar River and belonged to the Paddlers Band. Twice he joined war parties but was sent back each time because he was too young. He is now an elder of the Presbyterian Church.

Standing Rattle, 76 years, Oswego, Montana. Standing once made a trip with a war party but he has no war record. He was an Indian policeman for five years. Because he is a Medicine Man he sponsors the annual Medicine Lodge Dance. He was born near Poplar River and belonged to the Rock Mountain People Band. His son, Fire Bear, illustrated this book.

Duck, 79 years, Oswego, Montana. Duck was born near Scobey, Montana and belonged to the Paddlers of the Prairie Band. He was a famous warrior who went on nine war journeys and captured nine horses at different times. His war record includes the counting of a first coup, a second coup, the killing of an enemy, the taking of a weapon from an enemy and shooting into an enemy's camp. On October 5, 1877 he joined the United States Army in the war against the Nez Perce Indians. He was a member of the Indian Service for eighteen years. During this time he served as policeman, chief of police, and Judge of Indian Offenses.

Duck, Mrs., (wife of Duck), 78 years, Oswego, Montana. Mrs. Duck was born in North Dakota, the daughter of Chief Broken Arm of the Rock Mountain People Band. Her maiden name was Wing Woman.

Four Bull, 68 years, Oswego, Montana. Four Bull, who was born in north central Montana, belonged to the People of the Cold Band. He received his white name, James Roberts, when he enrolled in school in 1892.

Eagle Feather, 70 years, Frazer, Montana. Eagle Feather was born near Rock Creek, Montana. He was a member of the Ones That Go to the Dance Band. Although he had no Indian war record, he was at one time a member of the United States Army and was stationed at Fort Assiniboine from 1892 to 1895. He was an Indian policeman for two years.

Fire Moon, 76 years, Frazer, Montana. Fire Moon was born near the mouth of Muddy Creek, in the eastern part of the Fort Peck Reservation in Montana. He belonged to the Rock Band. He was outstanding among the Indians as a Medicine Man, who was privileged to participate in the Medicine Lodge Dance. He had no war record, but he was an Indian policeman for eleven years.

Crazy Bull, 77 years, Frazer, Montana. Crazy Bull was a famous warrior, whose deeds included a second coup, a fourth coup and the lifting of an enemy's scalp. He went on four war journeys and on October 5, 1877 joined the United States Army against the Nez Perce. Crazy Bull was born at Wolf Point, Montana, and belonged to the Paddlers of the Prairie Band.

Crazy Bull, Mrs., (wife of Crazy Bull), 87 years, Frazer, Montana. The maiden name of Mrs. Crazy Bull was Gray Back Woman. She was born at Fort Union and was a member of the Rock Band.

Red Dog, Mrs., 78 years, Frazer, Montana. Mrs. Red Dog was the wife of Chief Red Dog of the Red Bottom Band. She herself belonged to the Ones Who Stay Alone Band. She was born near Poplar, Montana.

Four Stars, Mrs., 74 years, Frazer, Montana. Mrs. Four Stars was born on Big Porcupine Creek in Montana. Her maiden name was Lodge Pole. She was a member of the Red Bottom Band.

Stands Shining, 70 years, Wolf Point, Montana. Stands Shining, who was born near Opheim, Montana, was an Indian scout for the United States Army. He participated in the driving of a band of Cree Indians from Montana across the Canadian line in 1893. He served in the United States Infantry at Fort Assiniboine from 1892 to 1896 and was discharged with the rank of First Sergeant. In 1929 he was ordained as a Presbyterian Minister. His white man's name is Chester A. Arthur. He was a member of the Rock Band.

Bear Rump, 75 years, Poplar, Montana. Bear Rump likewise acted as an Indian scout. He served at Fort Buford, North Dakota, in 1894. He was an Indian policeman for four years. Later he was in charge of Indian police and also acted as official interpreter until 1933 when he retired. His white name is Dan Mitchell. Bear Rump was born at White Earth, North Dakota and belonged to the Cree Speakers Band.

Martin Mitchell, 66 years, Wolf Point, Montana. Mitchell, a brother of Dan Mitchell, was born near Fort Belknap, Montana. He was a member of the Cree Speakers Band and is at the present time serving with the Indian police.

Shoots Them (Nick Alverz), 86 years, Wolf Point, Montana. Shoots Them, a member of the Rock Band, was born at Fort Union, Montana. He was a member of the United States Army expedition which marched into Chief Gall's Sioux camp south of Poplar, Montana, when Gall was taken prisoner January 2, 1881 and sent with his band on steamboats down the Missouri River to North Dakota reservations. At that time Shoots Them was an official interpreter for the Army.

Game Counter (Harvey Hamilton), 67 years, Wolf Point, Montana. Game Counter, a famous hunter and traveler, was a member of the Cree Speakers Band. He took part as a leader in the Ghost Dance religion of 1904 which swept westward among the Plains Indians. At present he is prominent in the activities of the Medicine Lodge Dance.

White Man, (also called Bobtail Bear), 71 years, Wolf Point, Montana. White Man was born in northeastern Montana and ranked as one of the best hunters of the Assiniboines. He is a leader in social societies, acting as official announcer. White Man was a member of the Paddlers Band.

Pointing Iron, 68 years, Wolf Point, Montana. Pointing Iron was born at Cypress Hills, Canada. His father was killed by Piegan Indians.

Dry Bone, 68 years, Santaluta, Saskatchewan, Canada. Dry Bone, in Canadian subject, was born near Fort Belknap, Montana. He was a member of the Paddlers of the Prairie Band.

One Claw, Mrs., 102 years, Frazer, Montana. Mrs. One Claw, a member of the Contrary People Band, was born at White Earth, North Dakota. Her maiden name was White Woman.

Stockade, 67 years, Frazier, Montana. Stockade, a prominent leader of the Assiniboine, represented his tribe at Washington, D. C. on four different occasions. He also served on the Tribal Council for three years. His white name is Walter Clark. He was educated at Santee Normal Training School in Nebraska.

Assiniboine Bands

James L. Long believes that this list of thirty-three bands, comprising the Assiniboine Nation, is the only complete one ever recorded.

Aegitina—Camp Moves to the Kill

Bizebina—Gophers

Cepahubi—Large Organs

Canhdada—Moldy People

Canhewincasta—Wooded-Mountain People

Canknuhabi—Ones That Carry Their Wood

Hudesabina—Red Bottom

Hebina—Rock Mountain People

Huhumasmibi—Bone Cleaners

Huhuganebabi—Bone Chippers

Hen atonwaabina—Little Rock Mountain People

Inyantonwanbina—Stone or Rock People

Inninaonbi—Quiet People

Insnaombi—The Ones Who Stay Alone

Indogahwincasta—East People

Minisose-Swnkeebi—Missouri River Dog Band

Minisatonwanbi—Red Water People

Osnibi—People of the Cold

Ptegabina—Swamp People

Sunkcebi—Dog Band

Sahiyaiyeskabi—Cree Speakers

Snugabi—Contrary People

Sihabi—Foot People

Tanidabi—Buffalo Hip

Tokanbi—Strangers.

Tanzinapebina—Owners of Sharp Knives

Unskaha—Roamers

Wadopabina—Paddlers

Wadopahnatonwan—Paddlers Who Live on the Prairie

Wiciyabina—Ones That Go to the Dance

Waziyamwincasta—People of the North

Wasinazinyabi—Fat Smokers

Wokpanbi—Meat Bag

Pronunciation Key:

ä, as in father

ȧ, as in sofa

ā, as in ale

ē, as in eve

ê, as in event

o͞o, as in food

ō, as in old

ȯ, as in obey

ch, as in church

g, as in go

n, (at the end of a syllable), as in French, bon soir

ħ, hard as in German

ʹ, a pause (not an accent)

There are four dialects in Dakota language, according to a dictionary compiled by John P. Williamson, A. M., D. D., and published by the American Tract Society of New York in 1911. These dialects are the Santee, Yankton, Teton and Assiniboine. Pronunciation of the Assiniboine words for the moons and seasons was obtained from *Dakota A B C Wopapi* by S. R. Riggs. This book was published by the Santee Normal Training School Press in 1929.

Pronunciation Guide for the Months and Seasons :

January—Wicogandu, Wē-chō-gän-dōo; also, witehi-wē-tä-hê
February—Amhanska, Äm-hän-skȧ
March—Wicinstayazan, Wēē-chē-shdä-yä-zän
April—Tabeȟawi, Tä-bä-ȟä-wē
May—Induwiga, In-dōo-wē´-gȧ
June—Wahpewosmewi, Wänȟ-bä-wō-shmä-wė́
July—Wasasa, Wä-shä-shä
August—Canpasapsaba, Chän-pä-säp-säb´-ȧ
September—Wahpegiwi, Wäȟ-bä-ghe-wė́
October—Tasnaheja-Hagikta, Tä-shnȧ-hä-jä–Hä-gē-ktȧ;
    also, Anukope, Ä-nōōk-ō´-pȧ
November—Cuȟotgawi—Chōō-ȟotgä´-wė́
December—Wicogandu-Sungagu, Wē-chō-gän-dōō–Sȯn-gä-gōō
Winter—Waniyedu, Wä´-nē-yä-dōō
Spring—Wedu, Wä-dōō
Summer—Mnogedu, M´nȯ-gä-dōō
Autumn—Pdanyedu, P´dan´-yä-dōō

Reading List

A list of other books for those who wish to know more about the Assiniboine:

Chittenden, Hiram M. *The American Fur Trade of the Far West.* A history of the Pioneer Trading Posts and Early Fur Companies of the Missouri Valley and the Rocky Mountains. New York, F.P. Harper, 1902, 3 v. frontis., plates, fold, map, facsims.

Denig, E.T. *Indian Tribes of the Upper Missouri.* 46th annual Report, United States Bureau of American Ethnology. Ed. with notes and biographical sketch by J.N.B. Hewett. Washington, D.C., Government Printing Office, 1930. illus., pl., ports., map.

Farnham, Thomas J. *Travels in the Great Western Prairies, the Anahuac and Rocky Mountains, and the Oregon Territory* and Father Pierre Jean de Smet, S.J., *Oregon Missions and Travels Over the Rocky Mountains in 1845–46.* Cleveland, Arthur H. Clark Co., 1906. 2 v. illus., plates, ports., maps, fold., plan, facsims. (vols. 28–29 of *Early Western Travels, 1748–1846,* ed. by Reuben Gold Thwaites).

Flagg, Edmund. *The Far West* and Father Pierre Jean de Smet, S.J., *Sketches, with a Narrative of a Year's residence Among the Indian Tribes of the Rocky Mountains.* Cleveland, Arthur H. Clark Co., 1906. 2 v. illus., plates, ports., maps, fold., plan, facisims. (vols. 26–27 of *Early Western Travels, 1748–1846,* ed. by Reuben Gold Thwaites).

Henry, Alexander and David Thompson. *New Light on the Early History of the Greater Northwest.* Manuscript journals of Alexander Henry, fur trader of the Northwest Company, and of David Thompson, official geographer and explorer of the same company, 1799–1814. Ed. by Elliot Coues. 3 v. New York, F.P. Harper, 1897. frontis., maps.

Larpenteur, Charles. *Forty Years a Fur Trader on the Upper Missouri.* Ed. by Elliott Coues. New York, F.P. Harper, 1898. 2 v. frontis., plates, ports., maps.

Lindquist, G.E.E. *Red Man in the United States.* New York, George H. Doran Co., 1923. frontis., illus., plates, ports., maps.

Lowie, Robert H. *The Assiniboine.* American Museum of Natural History, Anthropological Papers, Vol. IV, part 1. New York, American Museum, 1909. illus., front., plates.

MacLean, John. *Canadian Savage Folk.* Toronto, William Briggs, 1896. front., illus., port.

Maximilian, Prince of Wied. T*ravels in the Interior of North America, 1832–1834.* Cleveland, Arthur H. Clark Co., 1905. 4 v. illus., plates, facsims., map. (Vols. 22-24 of *Early Western Travels, 1748-1846,* ed. by Reuben Gold Thwaites.)

Owen, Major John. *The Journals and Letters of Major John Owen.* Ed. by Seymour Dunbar and Paul C. Phillips. New York, Edward Eberstadt, 1927. 2 v. pl., fronts., ports., facsims., maps.

Rodnick, David. *The Fort Belknap Assiniboine of Montana,* a Dissertation in Anthropology. Philadelphia, University of Pennsylvania, 1938.

Smet, Pierre Jean de. *Life, Letters and Travels of Father Pierre Jean de Smet, S.J., 1801–1873;* Missionary Adventures and Labors Among the Wild Tribes of the North American Indians, Ed. by Hiram Martin Chittenden and Alfred Talbot Richardson. New York, F.P. Harper, 1905. 4 v., frontis., plates, ports., map, facsims.

Wissler, Clark. *Indians of the United States.* New York, Doubleday, Doran Co., 1940. illus., plates, maps, appendix.

Writers' Project, Montana WPA. *Montana,* a State Guide Book. New York, The Viking Press, 1939, illus., maps.

More Native American History Titles

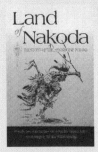

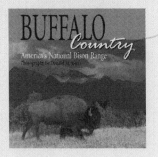

Available from your local bookstore or visit
riverbendpublishing.com or call toll-free 1-866-787-2363

RIVERBEND
PUBLISHING